The Possibility Exists ...

The Possibility Exists ...

Eoin Scolard

BOOKS

Winchester, UK
Washington, USA

First published by O-Books, 2016
O-Books is an imprint of John Hunt Publishing Ltd., Laurel House, Station Approach,
Alresford, Hants, SO24 9JH, UK
office1@jhpbooks.net
www.johnhuntpublishing.com

For distributor details and how to order please visit the 'Ordering' section on our website.

Text copyright: Eoin Scolard 2016

ISBN: 978 1 78535 524 0
978 1 78535 525 7 (ebook)
Library of Congress Control Number: 2016941418

A CIP catalogue record for this book is available from the British Library.

Design: Stuart Davies

Printed and bound by CPI Group (UK) Ltd, Croydon, CR0 4YY, UK

We operate a distinctive and ethical publishing philosophy in all
areas of our business, from our global network of authors to
production and worldwide distribution.

CONTENTS

Personal Contract

I, (Name) _____

understand that I am at the beginning of a journey which I may find challenging at times. I commit myself to complete self-honesty and to recognizing when I resist or attempt to derail my own growth. In recognizing this I fully commit myself to burn through any inner resistance I may encounter.

I understand that I will meet different aspects of myself along the way, and that I may be tempted to run away from what I find. Therefore I also commit to suspending all self-criticism, judgment and self-blame.

I choose to give this journey/project of self-exploration a meaningful name.

I shall call it:

_____

May I be guided, held and supported as it all unfolds.

Signed: _____

Date: _____

Dedication

I dedicate this book to the lovely Jenny, who has been my best friend, confidante, business partner, co-creator, lover and soulmate for the past seven years.

Thank you to my amazing four children, Ciaran, Conor, Aisling and Eimear, who taught me how challenging it is to love unconditionally. I'm still learning!

Thank you to my parents, Niamhin and Daithi, who brought me into this world and loved me.

Thank you to everyone in my life who supported me, got annoyed with me, spent time with me, loved me, disagreed with me and fought with me. You're all as much a part of this book as anyone else.

May the book make you laugh at my foolishness and surprise you and awaken you to the absolute delight of showing up authentically as yourself. May the world be a better place because of you.

Eoin Scolard
2016

Chapter 1

The Beginning

Lesson One
By the Ogre Known as Shrek

My favorite teachers are the most unlikely ones. Think musicians, comedians, children, animals – even movie characters. Remember our favorite ogre, Shrek, who decided to open up to Donkey as they began their adventure? Shrek believed he was a monster, because that's what people called him. But, after a while, he learned to ignore people's opinions of him. He told Donkey that there was a lot more to ogres than people saw. I love his famous line "Ogres are like onions" – and, of course, Shrek then holds out the onion to Donkey, who sniffs it.

"They stink?" says Donkey.

"Yes – well… No!" says Shrek.

Donkey goes on, "They make you cry?"

"NO!" says Shrek, "You just don't get it."

Shrek explained to Donkey that ogres were like onions because onions have layers, and ogres have layers too.

As Shrek later discovered, there's something underneath all those layers. That's what we're looking for. That's what we want to uncover and say "Hello" to. And along the way, we'll say "Goodbye" to layer after layer, just like Shrek.

Lesson Two
By the Sculptor Known as Michelangelo

Stay with me here as we jump from movies to history, from Shrek to Michelangelo. Remember him? The story goes that Michelangelo was asked about how he sculpted the famous statue of David, that now sits in the Accademia Gallery in Florence. It's said that he carved the statue out of a piece of marble that had been rejected by others. He said, "I focused my attention on the slab of marble, and then I chipped away at everything that wasn't David." You can't add to what's already perfect, so Michelangelo simply chipped away at everything that obscured the beauty he had glimpsed. Gradually, chip by chip, his wonderful masterpiece was revealed. That's what we need to do, me and you, because we're very similar in structure to that piece of marble. Yes, you might have some doubts about what's inside you, but I can tell you, from experience, that a great and raw beauty has been hidden inside you for a long time. It's the beauty of your own personal signature, which is your unique gift to the world. The world needs the real you, hidden away underneath, because the time for conformity and uniformity is over.

So it's time to say Goodbye to who you thought you were – and Hello to the You that exists underneath all your messed-up crazy ideas about yourself. Who told you that you're not enough? Who said you had to be more? Who said you had to strive, to achieve? Who said you have to have a well-defined purpose – a question many of my clients ask me. "What's my purpose?" they ask. My answer is very simple. "Your purpose," I say, as their eyes widen – "is to evolve. That's why you were born. All of life is evolving, so why not cooperate with that?"

Lesson Three
By Any Newborn Baby

Remember the last time you held a young baby and looked into those incredible eyes? What happened? Did you think, "Hey, little baby, you know what, you're just not enough as you are!" Or did you disappear into those deep pools, amazed by how beautiful a baby is because it's just itself, raw and undefended? Yes, you loved the baby just for... Being. 'Being' was enough – and it always is. Being is sacred, beautiful, precious – in itself, whether that's a baby, a flower, an adult, or you. Your BEING is enough. You saw that in the baby's eyes, but when was the last time you gazed at a flower that way? When was the last time you looked at an adult that way? Even more importantly, when was the last time you saw yourself that way?

The most important step you'll ever take is to see that. It's the Truth, with a Capital T. You've got to wake up to the Truth that there's nothing wrong with you. Evolution, or God if you like, has it handled, and all you need to do is cooperate. There is nothing wrong with you. There never was. That is the profound truth that all spiritual teachers have been pointing to for centuries. Yet most of us resist that possibility because we're so programmed to think otherwise. We think we lack something, and we spend most of our lives looking for it. The strange thing is that sometimes we don't even know what we're searching for but we do know that feeling of emptiness inside. It's like a gnawing in the pit of our stomachs – something is missing. We begin to build our personalities around this feeling of lack. We think we need to defend or hold onto what little we have. We defend our beliefs, our opinions, our money, our relationships. Without them, we have no idea who we are.

I see this over and over again when I ask people to sit opposite one another and look into each other's eyes for three minutes. Result? Most people are too scared to be seen. Why? Because, again, we think there's something fundamentally wrong with us, and we get scared that the other person will see that. So we don't connect with others, and therefore we don't deeply connect with our true selves – even though we want to. It's like we're off-course, and we know it, but we don't know how to get back on course. We're disconnected from our true self, and we 'invest' this disconnection in over-shopping, overeating, over-drinking, constant drama, blame, compulsive workaholism – anything to get away from that gnawing feeling.

But hang on a second! Let's go back to Michelangelo and his David sculpture. Underneath all that 'stuff' we've just talked about, there's a perfection, a beauty, an eternal essence that cannot be destroyed. Most of us have felt this at some time or another in our lives. You know that there's a place in you that longs to be found, longs to be touched and brought to life. To put it another way, there's a light inside you that longs to be seen. It also longs to reach out to others. It knows that it belongs somewhere but it doesn't know where. Getting to know this truth is about the most important thing any human can ever do. First you've got to open to the possibility that what I'm saying is true. Then you continue your normal everyday life while watching everything that gets in the way of that deeper essence. Something radical begins to happen. You're chipping away now, like Michelangelo, using all the material in your life, because you know that there's treasure underneath. One day you will find it, and, I promise you, your life will never be the same again. This treasure was likened to "the pearl of great price" – something that, once you find it, is worth more than all your earthly posses-sions. While you may still enjoy all that the earth has to offer (and please do!), you realize the utter insignificance of 'stuff' in the face of this pearl that you've found. You've come home and you finally belong.

This book is a radical encounter with everything that gets in the way of that discovery. In this book, I will tell you stories that will shock you sometimes, because most of us need to be shocked out of our complacency. I will be as open and authentic as I can be with you, sharing all my darkness, all my struggles, all my self-loathing, and all my light – and maybe even a touch of drama and artistic license! The reason I do this, and the reason I write this book, is twofold. First, it has simply demanded to be written. It's as if it birthed itself from underneath my own self-doubt. Second, my fervent wish is that it helps you, as it helped me in writing it, to meet your true Self. The Raw and Unapologetic You. Delicious You. Powerful You. Wise You. Vulnerable You. Authentic You.

So you will need to be like Michelangelo, chipping away

patiently at the layers that Shrek talked about, gradually revealing your own Being, your very own "pearl of great price." The world needs the real You. Nothing less will do because we're in an incredible transition right now, from the old to the new.

We are, as a species, beginning to wake up to the truth that we are an aspect of Consciousness itself, expressing through us. Consciousness (or God if you like) has always manifested in many different ways. Consciousness allows itself to birth again and again, in a huge variety of forms, all of which are implanted with the 'Impulse to Evolve' beyond their original state. The most evolved forms (that's us humans) are beginning to remember our true origin. Some of us can see that everything is a manifestation of the intelligence and love of Consciousness itself. Everything that is not aligned to this emerging Consciousness is being revealed. Truth is begging to be deeply valued. Authenticity wants to thrive in a way that it never has. Fear and Control-based social, political, religious and economic systems are crumbling as all Darkness is brought to Light. Those of us on the leading edge of cooperating with this 'Impulse to Evolve' know that we are Creators – and that together we are all capable of creating the New World.

The old establishments fear this emerging Consciousness because they're starting to lose their grip on our thinking. Some of them are clever enough to adapt and allow their structures to be transformed by encouraging their people to be authentically themselves, creating and cooperating as part of the new structure. Other companies, organizations and religions are dying off, some slowly and painfully, because their foundations are rotten, based on control, fear and greed.

The Internet revolution has connected every human being on the planet and opened up the concept of One World. This revolution is organic and unstoppable, because it transcends religion, race and nationality. It embraces difference and moves us beyond the old-style dualistic thinking of 'us and them.'

Borders, Boundaries and Control just won't function like they used to. A new paradigm is emerging and the foundations are Truth, Cooperation and Personal Responsibility.

To understand and cooperate with this emerging consciousness means that we have to leave the two-dimensional world behind. Our minds have been programmed to think in dualistic terms – 'black and white' – 'gay and straight' – 'I'm right, you're wrong.' Now we're being invited to transcend that old style of thinking. As the thirteenth century Sufi poet Rumi put it: "Out there beyond the concepts of right and wrong, there is a field. I'll meet you there." If he had our current metaphysical language, Rumi might have said that the field he was talking about was the quantum field where 'all things are possible.'

In this new space where all things are possible, we are beginning to recognize the limitations of the mind that is divided against itself. We cannot go on fighting with ourselves 'inside' because that's what we create 'outside.' Our internal struggles will always be mirrored externally in poverty, war, inequality and greed.

To move beyond duality we need to challenge our thinking and move into a new mindspace beyond our usual patterns of thought. This deeper Knowing cannot be simply conceptualized and stored away in our brains, side by side with our store of knowledge. It is NOT knowledge. It is something that is constantly emerging, changing and evolving – and therefore cannot be understood by the mind that wants to grasp, categorize and file away. Why? Einstein pointed towards this dilemma when he said, "You can never solve a problem on the level on which it was created." It's like trying to get yourself off the ground by pulling at your feet – you simply can't do it.

So that's the bad news I'm bringing you. While reading this book may help you to wake up, it's also an action book. I want you to move into a deeper 'Knowing,' and I'm firmly convinced that you cannot 'know' something until you have tasted it, touched it, smelled it, felt it and integrated it into the very fabric of your life. When you have an experience of something, no one can invalidate that experience. You simply know. That 'knowing' can be felt very deeply in the depths of your incredible body. Would you prefer to think about chocolate or experience it? While you may like the concept of chocolate, your experience of smelling it, tasting it and allowing it to melt in your mouth is a far deeper experience than just thinking about it.

So I invite you to accept that this book isn't a 'Self-Help' book. If you want to experience your true self, you need to recognize that this so-called 'Self' doesn't need help! It needs to be dismantled so that something new can emerge, something so deep and open, so inclusive, loving and creative that your mind can't grasp it. Yes, it involves practice, work and commitment. The commitment is that you honor your journey no matter how much resistance you feel or how many cul-de-sacs you go down. So I urge you to DO the things I recommend, and if a particular exercise really 'pushes your buttons' – great! It's perfect for you. At this level of engagement, there will always be resistance. Recognize it, accept it, embrace it – but don't let it win.

I'll leave the last words to Marianne Williamson, although they're usually attributed to Nelson Mandela because he used them in his inaugural speech:

Our deepest fear is not that we are inadequate. Our deepest fear is that we are powerful beyond measure. It is our LIGHT, not our darkness that most frightens us. We ask ourselves, Who am I to be brilliant, gorgeous, talented, fabulous? Actually, who are you not to be? You are a child of God. Your playing small does not serve the world.

There's nothing enlightened about shrinking so that other people won't feel insecure around you. We are all meant to shine, as children do. We were born to make manifest the glory of God that is within us. It's not just in some of us; it's in everyone. And as we let our own light shine, we unconsciously give other people permission to do the same. As we're liberated from our own fear, our presence automatically liberates others.

Chapter 2

Invitation To Italy

(The Journey)

If you're like most humans (and I guess you are if you're reading this) there's a deep longing inside you to be happy and fulfilled in all aspects of your life. Let's connect with that longing as we use a journey to Italy as an analogy. So you have a deep urge to go to Italy and you've probably known this for a long time. You've googled Italy and found out about Italian culture and history, the origin of the language, the food, the geography, the towns and the cities. You've ended up with lots of images and information about Italy. You can say, "Buon giorno" or "Arrivederci!" or "Ciao!" You've even bought Italian cookbooks and cooked a few tasty dishes, but you've never actually been to Italy! You may have looked at flights and places to stay but something has always stopped you from leaving where you are.

You've never touched the Italian soil! You've never smelled the aroma of the cities or laughed and jostled with a hundred Italians crammed into an early morning bakery. You've never experienced the espresso bars or heard the animated conversations in the most beautifully expressive language. You've never lounged in a piazza with a gelato in your hand and watched the men ambling arm-in-arm in the mid-morning sun. You've never sat underneath an olive tree or plucked a grape from the vine and read the language of love in the eyes of the young couples who are gesturing animatedly outside the cafe across the road. Sure, you've read it all. You've got lots of 'knowledge' about Italy and you may even talk about Italy as if you know it. But you don't know Italy. Why? Because you've never been there.

That's what it's like for most people. We're all interested in being happier and more conscious but deep down, we're all afraid to leave where we are. We're too comfortable, or too invested in our beliefs, our fears or even our misery. We don't really want to give up what we're accustomed to. I know this is still true for me now and then. I'm guessing it describes you too, at least some of the time. This fear of change seems to be a part of the current human condition. I remember M. Scott Peck in his famous book *The Road Less Travelled* saying that most people who came to him didn't want the truth. They just wanted relief. Even when we're unwell, we just want the tablet, the relief, the quick fix! We don't want the truth, which is this – THERE'S NO QUICK FIX. That's the truth, but it's also not a problem.

Why? Because you don't need a fix! What you need is this – to know that there isn't a problem. All your problems are lodged somewhere in your mind. Want proof? Take yourself and all the rest of us (humans) off the planet. Now tell me where the problems are. That's right. They don't exist anymore. They don't exist ON THE EARTH. They only exist IN YOUR MIND. And that is simply an understanding, a Truth with a Capital T. All problems begin and end in your mind. Period!

If you're still with me then I guess you're ready for a thrill or two as we dive deeply into the inner world. That way, we begin to make sense of our place in the outer world. Every now and then I may ask you to put this book down and do an exercise of some type. If you don't do the exercises and just keep reading then you probably won't get to Italy. It's your choice. Be very aware of that part of you that may activate at any time and decide to not really engage with this book. That part of you will sabotage your happiness as it may have done many times before. Remember that.

The reasons why we self-sabotage are extremely revealing but that's for later. For those of you who are committed to actually landing in Italy and tasting some fresh-made pasta, washed down by some gorgeous vino rosso and some delicious gelato, get ready to meet yourself in a new way.

If you haven't already done so, please go to the Personal Contract at the very beginning of the book. Read it and make sure you know what you're committing to. Then, as suggested, give the project a name and sign the contract. Last but not least – fasten your seat belt. We're about to take off!

Chapter 3

The Crazy-Making Mind

It is not that I'm so smart. But I stay with the questions much longer.
– Albert Einstein

Are we an intelligent species? Why do we even listen to thoughts like: "I'm not good enough" or "I can't do it" or "I should be better"? What causes us to hold onto thoughts like that and keep thinking them over and over again? What's the point of thoughts like that? It's as if someone else is in charge of what we think. That "someone else" is what we call the Ego-Mind – a hotchpotch of ideas, impressions and beliefs that sashayed their way into our lives when we were young children. This ego-mind is what you learned about who you are – from others, from experiences and from the society you grew up in. Crucially, however, it's not actually 'you.' It's only who you think you are – and there's a world of difference between that and your true self.

We need to be very courageous to allow ourselves to question our very sense of self and what we believe so that our deeper self, our authentic self, can shine through. What happens then is that you gradually trust that there's something incredibly loving and intelligent behind everything. This Knowing is way beyond the capacity of your mind. Your mind doesn't know how to take suns, planets and solar systems and hurtle them around galaxies. Your mind doesn't know how to make life happen. It can't comprehend that there was no beginning and that there is no end. It can't understand eternity because it lives in the dimension of time. Yet it's amazingly arrogant. It simply wants to believe what it believes, doesn't want to let go and is happy to stay in its own little bubble of consciousness.

That's what your current state of consciousness is like – a bubble. It's got a size and shape that defines it. It's easy to stay in your bubble but that will eventually get repetitious, boring and sterile. You believe what you believe and that's the way it is. There's millions of other bubbles floating around too. They all believe what they believe too. But wait! Our bubbles are floating around in something vast, spacious and open. We need to allow ourselves to open into that – into the immense world of limitless possibility, rather than stay stuck in our self-serving ego-minds.

It doesn't matter who you are or what you do – anyone can do this. Anyone can learn to dis-identify from their idea of who they are. What matters is that you trust that it's possible. It's a Knowing – not a thought, or a belief, or a religion. It's a way of living from your deepest self. Whether God exists or not doesn't concern you because, either way, it's just a belief. Nobody really knows anyhow! Yes, you may have convinced yourself that your version of God is the right one but YOU DON'T KNOW! Perhaps you are finally realizing, like many of us, that the mind-made world is quite insane at times. Yet you collude with it. You identify with it and so a part of you wants the insanity to continue. Why? Because you're afraid to let go.

Humanity is afraid. The mind-made ego-world that we've created is founded on fear. Politics, religions and the media sell us this fear – and we consume it. We buy things because of it. We have bought into fear itself. Businesses sell it to us every day. Who are you without it – without your fear? Who are you without something to worry about, moan about, fight against or stress about? Who are you without your possessions, your beliefs, your home, your role, your position? You're so attached to the idea of who you are, and who God is or is not, that you've lost touch with the real You. The 'God-You,' if you like. The You that can choose anything in any moment. The You that can create, with love, simply by allowing yourself to be You.

Most of us think we are the dancer. We're not. We're being

danced – by greed, by lust for power and control, by insecurity, by holding on or holding back, by needing to be approved of by others, by needing to be against something. These are all subtle forms of our need to be acknowledged. We think we're intelligent but we've forgotten how arrogant we are. We're listening far too much to our heads and not enough to our hearts. We're being danced by a subtle lie, called the Ego-Mind. Have a look at what it tells you, by filling out the first three things that come to mind. Be spontaneous!

My Most Dominant Negative Thoughts:

(About my body)

_____

_____

_____

(About someone that gets under my skin)

_____

_____

_____

(About life in general)

_____

_____

_____

When I first saw what was going on in my own mind, I was appalled, especially as I had my IQ tested at 147, in the top 3% of the population. I thought I was intelligent, a bright guy. I was able to solve problems, dabble in databases and write basic html. I have been an entrepreneur all my life. I can take risks. I can manage staff – though some of them might disagree! I can be very responsible and reliable. I really believed that I was intelligent until I began to question my own thoughts. After a while I realized that I wasn't so clever after all. LIFE came along and kicked me hard a few times over a ten-year period. It was as if I was being told, "You're deluded. You think you're smart, but look at you now. Where's all your cleverness now?"

One of those life kicks left me babbling on the floor of my home as I lost consciousness. Forty minutes later I was wheeled into Intensive Care in a Dublin hospital. Another time I remember lying in the middle of the floor during a weeklong retreat, crying my eyes out and not really knowing why. I thought I was falling apart. Nobody was able to console me. Every time I thought I had Life sorted and under control, I got a message from Life that said the opposite. Eventually (because I really am a slow learner), I found myself questioning everything I ever believed about love, relationship, family, success, what was right and what was wrong.

LIFE showed me many things including the fact that I was invested in beliefs that just didn't work for me anymore. My supposed 'Intelligence' wasn't working for me. A part of me knew that I needed to make some big changes in my life but I wasn't listening to that part. I kept on doing the same things over and over until, surprise, surprise! I realized that, over and over, I was getting the same results! Hmmm. Finally it came to me – I was the common denominator in every situation. As you've gathered by now, I'm not such a bright guy after all!

After those serious wake-up calls, along with my powerful near-death experience, I began to doubt my own propaganda. Did

I really have a high IQ? Was it intelligent to think so negatively about myself? Was it intelligent to be cut off from my emotional world? Was it intelligent to drink seven coffees a day? Was it intelligent to do things just to make people like me? Was it intelligent to hate some of my own thoughts? Was it intelligent to think I was bad and defective in some way? Was it intelligent to always avoid conflict even if it meant denying my own truth? Was it intelligent to stay in a relationship which wasn't good for me?

I seemed to lack the basic intelligence of how to care for myself in healthy ways. I had no idea what my deep needs were. I had no idea how to love myself. What chance had I then of really loving another? I had no idea how to be happy. After many years of counselling, healing, psychotherapy and lots of other strangely wonderful experiences, I realized that I had been missing something really important. I didn't find it overnight but I can honestly say that, over a 15-year period, I did find something. It transformed my whole life – from the inside out. I learned how to say Hello to ME. All of ME. I learned to open. I learned to sit with pain (mine and others') without trying to fix it. I learned all about my defense mechanisms, my projections and my shadow. I learned how to hold – and how to let go. I learned how to set healthy boundaries. I learned to not blame others for being themselves. I learned to notice all the energy I was wasting and then I learned how to reclaim it. I learned how to feel all my emotions unconditionally because they were mine. I learned how to be at peace with ALL THAT IS.

As all this developed I began to deepen in love with me, then with others, then with life. Many teachers and courageous souls accompanied me along the way. The journey has been revelatory, as it will be for you. It has cracked me open – and that's a good thing. I needed to be cracked open. A lot of us do.

Looking back now, over 15 years later, it all seems strangely surreal, as if I'm looking back at a different person in a different life. Back then I was a successful businessman with a great life –

according to many people! I had read lots of self-help books and understood the power of positive habits and how to 'succeed.' The truth, however, was that I lived inside a cocooned idea of who I was. That idea of who I was had been shaped by others. I had no deep connection to my true self. While I had a strong self-image, that's all it was – a self-image – or an 'image of self' if you like. It certainly wasn't the real me!

I had become a master at pretense, hiding my fears and low self-esteem behind a projected outer layer of confidence. My passive-aggressive personality was also hidden away, buried by the internalized belief from my childhood programming: "I don't do conflict – because I'm a good person." I showed everyone how happy I was and how sure I was of myself and my place in the world. It was too scary and vulnerable to let people see what was really going on. I didn't want to admit to the world that I was full of fear, and that I didn't feel good about me. I didn't want to admit to myself that my life had started to crumble, and that I had started hearing a voice whispering inside me!

Listening to that voice was the best thing I've ever done. It was that inner voice that we all have. It whispers things you know to be true, but you ignore them. In my case, it took me by the hand and dragged me, coaxed me, little by little, into having an honest look at myself. It eventually brought me to a place where I found everything I wanted – inside. It was so strange to realize that there was nothing wrong with me. It was humbling to find out that all my striving was an attempt to build a new 'better' me that people could admire. My ego-mind was in charge all that time, reinforcing my belief that that I wasn't enough. Somebody wise once said to me, "You know, people rejected Jesus 2,000 years ago – not because he brought 'good news' – but because he brought NEW news. We don't like the NEW if it challenges the OLD." I can see this truth very clearly now. Your mind likes to hold on. It doesn't like the new when it challenges the old.

It's true. Try it. Take something you believe to be true and try to think the opposite. Take the thought "Life is difficult" and change that to "Life is a breeze!" Not so easy, huh? When you encounter any resistance within you to a new way of thinking the simplest way through it is to invoke the childlike energy of CURIOSITY. Whatever we find is OK. Just be curious about it all. In my classes and workshops I like to ask people to remember the curiosity they experienced as children. We were curious about everything, and that curiosity helped to open up the external world to us. In fact, curiosity was totally necessary. Now let's use that capacity to be curious about our internal world. Be curious about why your mind wants to get involved and run a commentary on you, your body, your life and everyone else's life. Be curious about what your mind thinks and why it thinks it.

I remember a particular incident at work when I reacted very strongly because my boss changed his mind about something important that we had agreed on. I snapped at him and I told him what I thought of him and his morals (or lack of them, to be precise!). We ended up having a major disagreement. He was shocked. He didn't know that I was a little shocked too. It seems that I had been stoking the fires of resentment for a long time!

When the anger had subsided, I felt really bad about losing my cool, but I also felt good about standing up for myself! I was curious about my passionate reaction. Why hadn't I been able to feel my anger in a healthier way? Why couldn't I communicate more clearly? I saw a few things straightaway. I saw that I had been holding back from speaking honestly a long time. I saw that I was feeding an old pattern of resentment towards him simply because I perceived him to be too confident and too full of himself. I often spoke to others about him but I never spoke directly to him. And so I learned that I was passive-aggressive and that I didn't know how to communicate my anger directly. I had to let the anger out by talking about him but not directly to him. As I looked more closely at this pattern I began to see that I had a choice – either continue to feed my resentment or realize that I was somehow afraid to speak my truth and do what I needed to do. Once I faced into this fear I saw that a part of me wanted to be 'full of myself' too! I resented his power because it showed me that I had not claimed my own power. I had given it away, and fed my powerlessness and resentment instead. I was classic passive-aggressive. This was a real shock to me!

Problem No. 1
We Think Too Much, Too Quickly.

How many thoughts do you have per day? A Harvard study came up with a figure of roughly 50,000 – every day! Most of them are fleeting. Most of them are negative. Lots of them are hardwired into our psyche and so we repeat the same thoughts over and over again. We're not taking anything new in. When we're reading a new self-help book we skim over the words and never really connect with what's being offered. It's easy to read any book without it having any lasting impact.

We're a bit like seabirds skimming the waves. We're just scanning, looking for something interesting. We like to flit around and look interested, but we're not too sure about actually diving in. But if the bird didn't fold its wings, take aim, and dive in, it would starve. We're no different. We need to dive in too – because most of us are starving.

OK, so maybe we can live without fish, but we are starving for depth, experience and real fulfilment. We want to feel more alive but we don't know how. There's that constant nagging in our minds telling us that there's something missing – but that's where we encounter our next hurdle.

Problem No. 2
Our Minds Have Convinced Us That There's Something Missing.

As you know, your mind has its own storehouse of opinions, beliefs and judgments. It loves to feed them, to defend and preserve them too as if there is something original about them! So, when you read a book like this, your mind gets really involved. It has convinced you that there's something missing. So it needs you to 'seek' – to seek out more information and then, when it finds something, it adds that to your storehouse of knowledge. So you pick up a book like this and read something new. Straightaway your mind says, "Oh, that's a lovely new concept, I like that. I'll add it to my storehouse, stick a mental label on it, and file it away."

It's easy to become a magpie in this new world, picking up the shiny bits that you like and storing them away. That's what the mind loves to do – seek, and keep seeking!

You know that old saying "seek and you shall find"? Well, I have news for you. The mind doesn't want us to "find" anything. It wants to "seek and NOT find." Why? Well, think about it this way. Once your mind stops seeking, what will it do? If you didn't believe that there was something missing, what would your mind do? It would begin to lose power, because your sense of identity would not be bound up in 'seeking' anymore. You might find yourself realizing that there's nothing wrong with you and that there's nothing to seek for. Do you think your mind wants that to happen? No, of course not. It has many strategies in place to make sure you do not 'find.'

So, straightaway, we are presented with both problems. The first problem is that we tend to think too quickly, skimming over everything. The second problem is that our minds may be sabotaging the very thing we long for. Here's two simple solutions – and they're so simple, your mind may resist them. (That's how cunning it is!)

Solution 1
Slow Down. Stop. Breathe.

First off – slow down the pace of your reading. Take it a paragraph at a time. If something resonates with you, stay with it for a while. Don't try to get to the end of the page, never mind the end of the book. If there is an exercise that needs to be done, please do it before you move on. Otherwise you're just feeding your mind with yet more concepts. You're also feeding your normal behavior pattern of rushing through things. If you feel yourself resisting this invitation then that's your mind at work again. Be aware of that resistance and what it's saying. Go deep into it and see it for what it is – the ego-mind desperately trying to ensure you don't uncover its secrets and strategies for survival. So, welcome the resistance – it shows you're on to something!

Solution 2
Develop A Felt Sense.

Secondly, get a FEEL for what I'm trying to communicate rather than using your mind to take a position on it. Please don't try to reason it all out. There is no need to believe anything, just as there is no need to disbelieve. Simply listen, with your heart and body. Develop a 'FELT SENSE' of what is true for you, even though your mind may say, "That's not rational," or "That doesn't fit." Put yourself in a state of curiosity as you read this book. Put your hand on your heart and let it be in charge for a while. Tell your opinionated mind to get lost! These are just suggestions for you. Do whatever works for you – but you've got to move into curiosity and openness. If something I write doesn't make 'sense' – SLOW DOWN. STOP. BREATHE. When you find yourself skimming – SLOW DOWN. STOP. BREATHE.

If you find yourself reacting to something I say, SLOW DOWN. STOP. BREATHE. If you find yourself rushing, SLOW DOWN. STOP. BREATHE. Then tune into yourself and FEEL what's happening inside you. Remember that your ego-mind is built for survival. It will attempt to sabotage any change, whether that's by rushing on through, or by ignoring or resisting. Notice that. Be aware of any patterns of sabotage – and keep being curious about your reactions, whatever they are. The more you do this, the more you land in this deeper 'felt sense' within you. Remember the child you once were, the child who was oh-so curious and oh-so inventive and oh-so spontaneous. That child is still here inside you. That curiosity is still there along with the creativity and the inventiveness. The playfulness and the spontaneity is still inside you. Remember that as you read on because you will encounter resistance and self-sabotage. It happens to all of us so don't condemn yourself when they arise. Be curious and playful about your own resistance to change.

Rumi wrote a wonderful poem about this journey into self. When you read it, don't skim. Dive into the words!

The Guest House
(by Jalaluddin Rumi)
This being human is a guest house.
Every morning a new arrival.
A joy, a depression, a meanness,
some momentary awareness comes
as an unexpected visitor.
Welcome and entertain them all!
Even if they are a crowd of sorrows,
who violently sweep your house
empty of its furniture,
still, treat each guest honorably.
He may be clearing you out
for some new delight.
The dark thought, the shame, the malice,
meet them at the door laughing and invite them in.
Be grateful for whatever comes.
because each has been sent
as a guide from beyond.

The poem outlines our task if we're to embrace life in all its fullness, including all of ourselves – and all of 'what is.' We need to embrace the present moment, in anything that arises – whether it's fear, negative thinking, apathy, resistance, or any life situation or story that would pull us off-track. To embrace 'what is' does not mean that you succumb to it or let it take you over in any way. Let's take negative thinking as an example. To embrace 'negative thinking' means that you include it in your awareness – simply because it's there.

When you meet someone socially you probably say Hello, or something similar. You're simply acknowledging that the person is here. It's the same when you find anything in your inner world. Say Hello to whatever you find. If you encounter negativity, say, "Hello negativity." Don't tell yourself, "I shouldn't think negative thoughts," because now you're rejecting what is – and you're also feeding the pattern of self-rejection. So don't allow your mind to say, "I should" or "I shouldn't." Simply notice that self-rejection is a part of your inner dynamic, but don't allow that self-rejection to perpetuate itself. Say Hello to that too! ("Hello Self-Rejection.") Embrace it as part of your conditioned self and continue to watch the negativity in your mind. It can become a game for you – Spot the Negativity! That's the type of attitude we need when we start exploring our inner world.

Many years ago I watched Keanu Reeves as Neo in the movie *The Matrix*. Neo believes he's living a normal enough life as a computer programmer for a software company. In the evenings, he's a hacker. He lives alone, doesn't sleep much and feels a profound emptiness in his life. It's something he can't put his finger on – until he is contacted by Trinity. "It's the question that drives us," she whispers in his ear. That resonated with me. There's a question underneath all our pain, stress and wound-edness. The question varies from "Is this all there is?" to "How did I get here?" to "Who am I?" We need to honor those questions and open up to them, as Neo did.

Later on, Neo is repeatedly asked, "Are you the One?" Some think he is, some aren't sure, and some doubt, but all of them are left wondering about it. All, that is, except for Morpheus, who has no doubt. He proclaims to Neo, "You are the One." In this book I am saying the same thing to you. You are the One you've been waiting for. Are you ready for that?

My own experience has shown me again and again how easy it is to be diverted away from that which we long for and to fall back into familiar patterns. When I got to the point where I knew that I was 100% free to choose my own way of being in the world, I met another barrier – the fear of being truly authentic, of being completely me! I knew that I was the One – and that no person, no success or failure – in fact nothing at all – could take away from that truth. Then I realized that I was afraid of who I REALLY was – without my personal story, without my beliefs, successes and failures, without my past. I struggled with that realization for a few months. It was a very strange time. Somehow, I was afraid of the real me! I was afraid of how powerful I could be. I was afraid of how creative I could be. I was afraid of how vulnerable I could be. I was afraid of how honest I could be. I was afraid... of how others would react to this new me.

I began to ask myself, "Why am I afraid?" and "What am I really afraid of?" They were powerful questions and they awakened a deeper awareness in me. Questioning your mind is very powerful. Questions like this opened me up – to something which shocked me! Part of me was used to playing small and powerless sometimes. That part of me quite liked talking about and blaming others! I had normalized this version of me and, of course, it kept playing out in my life over and over again.

When you're used to playing small in a particular part of your life it's very challenging to really step up to the mark and be the best possible version of yourself. It's quite challenging to own your power and your own greatness. Somewhere along the line I had learned that it was easier to play safe, follow the unspoken rules and stay small. I associated that with humility. Bad move!

I eventually learned that everyone has the right to be whatever they choose to be and that there was nothing humble about letting others shine while I grumbled about them, resented them and bitched about them. That was my payoff. So it's really important to be honest with yourself. You may even be at the point where you're quite comfortable with the concept of being the best possible version of you – but it may still be just a concept. Have you really taken responsibility? Can you look back over your life and recognize all the times you abdicated your greatness or denied your intuition – and still forgive yourself? Can you look inside and recognize that a smaller version of you wants to live on, pointing the finger at others through judgment, resentment, blame or 'poor me' energy? Can you recognize that an equally powerful part of you is crying out for you to take full responsibility for every choice you made in the past and for every choice you will make from this moment on? Can you see all that and still be aware that it's the greater part of you that's seeing it all? Can you open up to the depth of your magnificence?

That is the vision I have for this book – that you might learn to open up to your own magnificence and let it shine through every aspect of your life. You have something to offer the world, but you've got to peel back all the layers that cover it up. When Michelangelo was asked how he sculpted, he is reported to have said that he "released" David from the block of marble. "I chipped away, bit by bit, at anything that wasn't David." That's the process here, to release you. My mission is to educate you and give you the tools to do that, to chip away, bit by bit, working with the circumstances of your life – to uncover the magnificent You that's already there waiting to be revealed.

Beliefs

As in Rumi's poem, remember to acknowledge anything that arrives as a "friend" who has taken up temporary accommodation in your house. Get used to seeing your beliefs in the same way – they have temporary residence only. They will all eventually leave. However, all of your beliefs have an overall protector, whose voice will try very hard to convince you of things like, "This book is not for you," or "You've read so many books – nothing really helped. Why would this be any different?" or simply "Why don't you just skip ahead." This voice will sound as if it's for your own good – but it's not. It's a psychological phenomenon called the super-ego that arises whenever we begin to confront our ideas of who we think we are. I heard the wonderful Miranda MacPherson, founder of the Interfaith Seminary in London, describe it as a psychic condom. It's like a skin that you've grown to keep all your beliefs about yourself and about everything under wraps. The great Indian sage Ramana Maharshi put it like this: "It's like a thief dressed as a policeman pretending to guard the treasure."

We think that our beliefs are the treasure, because we've identified with our beliefs. We get very frightened whenever we start to question our own beliefs. We don't want to let them go because our identity is bound up in our beliefs. Who are we without them? Who indeed? When we question our ideas of who we are, we often feel like we're falling apart. In a way, that's a true statement. We are falling apart but it's a healthy falling apart. The old has to make way for the new. Nothing bad is happening, even though it may feel that way sometimes.

Remember, too, that any belief you encounter within yourself is only that – a belief – and a belief is simply a thought that you have been thinking for a very long time. You really need to understand that. A belief is simply a thought that you have been tuned into for a very long time.

It's a bit like holding a TV remote control in your hand. You sit down on the couch, grab the remote control and select your favorites. Then you select the channel you want, and then the program you want to tune into. You press the button and you activate the download through your satellite dish. You're pulling a data stream from a satellite way up there in the atmosphere, and your dish is receiving the signal – and then converting it into images which jump onto the TV screen. It's remarkable really, but we take it for granted and don't think too deeply about it.

One day, I had a mini Aha! moment when I realized that we all have a remote control in relation to our thoughts. Our thoughts are the same as the packets of information that stream down from the satellite through our dish and into our TVs, or from the cloud onto our computers. That's what thoughts are – packets of information. They aren't actually held inside our heads. They come and they go. It's as if we download our thoughts from way out there somewhere, just like we activate our TV channels via satellite or the Internet. Unfortunately, some of us don't even realize that we have a choice. We seem to be always switched on to a particular channel, like the 'Drama Channel' or the 'Anxiety Channel,' or even the 'Not Enough Channel.'

I imagine that the programming might look like this:

Drama Channel
15:00 Comparison Crackers!
Meet the people who seem obsessed with comparing themselves to others. They say that others have it easy or have it made. We go on a journey to find these others. Will we find them? Do they exist?
17:00 What happened to me in the past (repeat)
A boring story that has been repeated over and over again. Wallow in it with us for the 23rd time!
18:00 You won't believe what he said!
You really won't! It's incredible. He said all kinds of things. Amazing!
Not Enough Channel
20:00 There's never enough time
Join Deborah and Jeremy as they talk to people who are

always so busy that they never have time for themselves. They have turned from human beings into human doings!

21:00 There's not enough money

We investigate why it is that we never seem to have enough money. We found lots of people who like to talk a lot about not having enough.

22:00 There's not enough love

A provocative look at the lives of people who are bitter about the lack of love in the world. We wonder if they are only getting what they give out?

Anxiety Channel

17:30 Something bad is going to happen soon.

Join us as we conjure up what might happen in the future. Yes, we know it's fiction, but it just might happen. We prepare for all the worst eventualities.

18:30 The News

A roundup of all the national and international stories of the day, focusing on negativity, problems, atrocities and everything bad in the world.

OK, that was me being creative! But it's good to have a laugh at ourselves sometimes and not take it all too seriously. We are constantly streaming and downloading different programs with our minds. What channel are you hooked into?

It may be a strange thing to say but lots of us are watching the same channels. It's as if our precious thoughts are not even our own. Most of them are negative and recurring, over and over again. It's like you don't even realize that you're beaming them in. You haven't noticed the remote control in your hand, and even if you do, you never think of changing the channel. You haven't realized that the TV is always on and that you have the power to switch it off!

So now you have three components in the thought process. You have the packets of information up there somewhere, you have the satellite dish and you have the remote control. The packets of information (thoughts) are always floating around, and they tend to gather together just like TV channels. Thoughts tend to band together in what we call group or tribal consciousness. When we belong to a particular group we tend to tune into the normalized thoughts of that group.

So, for instance, if you're a woman who was raised Catholic, you were tuned into the normalized thoughts of women who were brought up as strict Catholics. You may not have realized that you're always tuned into that particular channel. Why is that? Because your thinking has become so habitual that you believe you are your thoughts. People say things like, "I am a Catholic" or "I am an agnostic." Both statements are untrue. If we were to unpack the first of those thoughts we would find that what's really going on is this – "I was born into a Catholic family, and the authority figures in my life told me I was Catholic. My mind began to think Catholic thoughts and after a while that became my normal way of thinking. At some point I stopped realizing that I was the one doing the thinking, and I began to believe that my thinking was actually me!"

This is what is called identification. We identify with our thoughts – in other words, we think we ARE OUR THOUGHTS. Someone says something to you, and your mind feels threatened. It thinks, "That wasn't so nice. I'm under attack." That's why you react, even though nothing is actually happening. There's no danger at all and nobody is under attack. When you look at thoughts in this way it becomes clear that your thinking is not 'real' in the ultimate sense.

When you get used to having that remote control in your hand you will begin to choose your channels carefully. You may even begin to change your favorites, so that you are only beaming in what actually works for you. Finally, you may have an AHA! moment and realize that you can turn the TV off altogether. When you can do that on a regular basis – take the remote control and turn the TV off – you've arrived at an even deeper level of being. This is the place we call "No-mind."

> All you can do now is to relax into this nothingness... Fall into the silence between the words... watch the gap between the incoming and outgoing breath... and treasure each empty moment of the experience. Something sacred is about to be born.
> Osho, *The Transcendental Game of Zen*

For now, though, please remember that while any thought can be changed the negative ones want to get in. They want 'you' to keep thinking them all the time – that's how they get to 'live.' Here's the way I see it. A thought is 'out there' – until you switch your remote on and tune into it. Once you tune in often enough, it becomes hardwired into your consciousness and forms a belief. You've effectively downloaded it, and it stays attached to you until you challenge it.

Here's a few common core beliefs you may encounter:

1　I don't deserve... (Fill in the blank.)
2　I'm not... enough. (This one is clever because it's self-fulfilling.)
3　It never works out for me. (Sucks you down into self-pity.)
4　I know I've started this but I won't finish it. (Usually a subtle one, in the background.)
5　I don't have enough time for this... (This one is strong on self-justification.)
6　This is pointless... (This one kicks in when you're having a low day.)
7　I can't do this... (This one pulls you into powerlessness.)

When I encounter some pesky beliefs I often use the following practice. I sit down for a minute, take a few deep breaths and sense into the lower half of my body. Then I say to myself – "I am like an oak tree." Then I use my right brain to imagine myself as an oak tree, with roots going deep into the earth. The sun is high in the sky and I'm warm and toasty. Mmmm. If you're going to do this, then paint the scene vividly, because you're going to return to it time and again throughout your journey. What size are you, the oak tree? Are you in a forest or a field, or part of a hedge running along a road? What season is it?

Now take the particular belief you're working on and give it the name of a cartoon character. Let's try Mickey Mouse this time around. The belief can be any belief, so let's use one which most of us share – "I'm not good enough." These words are on the front of the T-shirt that Mickey Mouse is wearing. If you can see those words and hear him talking away, then obviously you can't be the thought or belief. It's not you. It's just Mickey Mouse. You're the one who's watching and listening! Acknowledge this cartoon representation of your thought or belief by waving at him. It's as if you're saying, "Hello, Mickey Mouse, I hear you and see you. I see you want my attention. Sorry, not today!"

When I've acknowledged Mickey (the thought or belief), I then turn my attention back to my roots, the earth below me and the sun and sky above me. I sense into the depth of the earth, how strong and solid it is. I feel into the warmth of the sun, the openness of the sky and the vastness of the universe. I notice that Mickey Mouse is getting annoyed with me. This belief "I'm not good enough" wants my attention, but I'm not giving it any. As I give it less and less attention, it gets more and more frantic and its voice gets higher and higher. By not engaging with it you're now starving it of the attention it needs to feed on. Attention to any thought gives it energy. Putting your attention elsewhere starves the thought of its life energy, which was coming from you.

When we consistently 'feed' a thought, it literally gets heavier and heavier until it becomes a hardwired belief. It drops deeper and deeper into the psyche. Conversely, if you simply acknowledge the thought and watch it – but don't 'feed' it – it loses energy. It starts to feel less dense. It gets lighter and lighter. It needs your attention or energy, either by believing it or by fighting it, but now you're not playing the game anymore. Poor Mickey Mouse! You see him getting lighter and lighter and then smaller and smaller, as he starts to float up and away. You see him passing through the clouds now, and all of a sudden he's gone. You're still the oak tree. You're still connected to the solidity of the earth below you, and the vastness of the sky above. Yes, there are clouds up there. They are all the negative thoughts. Yes, the weather (belief patterns) changes and storms (times of chaos) will come but you're watching it all now, knowing your own strength and depth as an oak tree. When a storm comes, you don't have to fight it. You simply let it blow through. When this becomes a regular practice, you may find that the weather patterns, and even the climate, have changed dramatically!

This is a very simple exercise. Get used to the idea that you're able to watch all the crazy cartoon characters in your mind, coming and going, wanting your attention. Stay as an oak tree. Acknowledge them, maybe with a wave of a branch, but don't engage in debate or argument. Remember that our cartoon characters want to pull us away all the time – into drama, negativity, self-doubt, blame – and so on. As you develop this way of looking at your beliefs, you will gradually create a little bit of distance between you and them. That's what we want. You are becoming 'non-attached.' This is the beginning of freedom.

Let's move on now to an exercise to show you what goes on in your mind. Fill in the blanks yourself in these three sentences – spontaneously. Don't censor yourself. Don't overthink it. Write it down and then move on to the next one. You may be surprised what you find. We'll come back to what you've written in a little while.

I SHOULD

_____

_____

_____

_____

I'M NOT

_____

ENOUGH.

I'M WORRIED THAT

_____

Many of us process information in a consistently negative or biased way. NLP (Neuro-Linguistic Programming) has discovered that "neurons that fire together wire together." This means that, based on our experiences of life up until now, we have hardwired all kinds of beliefs into our emotional and physical worlds without even being aware of most of them. It can be quite tricky to get in touch with beliefs that are hardwired into your system. Often they are so ingrained in your psyche that you can't see them, and you may need support. Here's an example from a client I worked with a few years ago who had great difficulty in her relationships with men.

Claudia (not her real name) was a very successful career woman but she couldn't seem to attract the right man. During our second session together we tried something new, having centered and grounded ourselves for ten minutes at the beginning. Then I asked her to keep eye contact with me, in silence, for three minutes, and to allow herself to connect with me in that way.

After about 30 seconds she starting joking about what we were doing and we had a giggle together.

Then I gently asked her to notice that her giggling was a manifestation of a nervousness. We resumed the practice of not speaking for a further three minutes. This time she got past the minute mark and began to allow herself to feel the impulse to break away, but (and this is important) she didn't give in to the impulse to speak or giggle. All of a sudden she began to cry as she connected in with a part of her which deeply distrusted men. She had never been aware of that distrust within her psyche but there it was. Her father had left her mother when she was five years old, and she had never understood the impact that was still having on her. Her vulnerable five-year-old mind had fired up a whole bunch of assumptions about men and how it wasn't safe to need them or rely on them, let alone love them, because they could leave you at any time.

While she had experienced many relationships as an adult, Claudia had always found a way of sabotaging every relationship so that she didn't have to commit deeply. That was her strategy for not getting hurt again, but it also meant that she never attracted the kind of man she REALLY wanted. Her neurons fired up the same message each time she started a relationship, warning her not to get too involved. Naturally enough, the type of men she did get involved with were men who wouldn't commit and weren't to be trusted. They let her down. They abandoned her or cheated on her, and all of that reinforced this belief pattern that was at work within her. Basically it said, "Men can't be trusted so don't open your heart to any man. Whatever you do, don't let your guard down."

In Claudia's case the important first step had been taken. It's this. You need to get to know what scripts are running inside you. The event of her dad leaving had left a deep wound within Claudia's psyche and so she had a number of scripts running. Her first script was "Don't trust men." That resulted in a few other 'subplots' such as "Don't let your guard down" and "I'm not loveable." Her mind had decided that her dad wouldn't have left if she (Claudia) was loveable. On a deeper level she even believed that she was somehow responsible for him leaving. When we believe we're not loveable we will sabotage those relationships that are good for us. We will also hold onto relationships that are not good for us and will accept second-best. Some of us will even tolerate physical and psychological violence.

It takes a commitment (and patience) to develop this deeper awareness. We need to notice any thought patterns which reinforce fear, lack or low self-esteem. Once we've done that, the traditional route is to start thinking more positively, to use affirmations and to challenge the negative. While these approaches can be useful, I prefer a more radical one, and it's this... STOP IDENTIFYING WITH YOUR MIND. Remember that the script has not been written by you – it's simply an energetic response to your life experiences. Just because your mind is trying to replay the same old stuff doesn't mean that it's YOU. It's just your MIND. If you can recognize that your mind is trying to recreate thoughts which reinforce your fears, negativity and so on, you've taken an important first step. There's now a part of you (your mind) that's trying to recreate the same thoughts – and there's this other part of you that's aware of what's happening. Stay with the part that's aware. Breathe into it and get familiar with it. This will help you to dis-identify from your mind. Notice then that your mind will put pressure on you to come back into its grip. It wants your attention. Why? Because without 'you,' your mind has no power. It will pull you back in with words like NEVER, ALWAYS, SHOULD or SHOULDN'T, CAN'T, MUST, ENOUGH. But now you can notice the energy of these thoughts. Notice how they want to make you feel powerless, fearful, stressed, defective or wrong in some way.

I remember a client (let's call him Jim) saying to me, quite strongly, "Hang on a second, Eoin. I really SHOULD get to the gym more often. That's a positive thought, isn't it?" Gently I asked him to FEEL INTO his reaction to the "SHOULD" thought, and he finally agreed that, "I really SHOULD get to the gym more often," stressed him. The more he allowed the thought, "I should get to the gym more often," the worse he felt about himself. I then asked him why he kept thinking he should go to the gym more often. His answer? "Because I don't want to be overweight and unfit." OK, I said, that's usually what a negative mind will do – it will focus on WHAT YOU DON'T WANT (which was to be overweight and unfit) – and that will result in you feeling bad about the situation. But there's no real power in there because the motivation to go to the gym is fear-based. The motivation is: "If I don't go to the gym then I'll be overweight." The thought is not there to motivate you – it's there to put you down. Result? Less energy. Less motivation. More self-attack.

I developed a technique which my clients say helps them a lot. It's very simple. Put the phrase, "My mind says that" before the thought. So I asked Jim to change the narrative. This is what I want you to do too. Every time you think, "I" – change it to "My mind says that I…" In this example, Jim changed, "I should get to the gym" to "My mind says that I should get to the gym." Notice the difference. It's more impersonal. It's more removed. You're not so strongly identified with it. Keep seeing it as separate from you, like a thought that's floating around in the sky.

Now let's go back to the examples that I asked you to fill in earlier. The first one was: "I SHOULD _____" Let's apply the technique of changing the "I" to "My mind says that." I'm going to use a familiar one: "I should lose some weight."

Notice how the thought makes you feel. Pretty bad, huh? Now replace the "I" with "My mind says that" – as in "My mind says that I should lose some weight." Now you can be interested in that statement, as in, "Really? My mind says that? It sounds critical to me. I wonder why my mind is criticizing me. It doesn't really help. If I keep on thinking that thought, I will feel really frustrated at myself, and possibly even depressed."

Here's the second example: "I'M NOT _____ ENOUGH." Using our non-attachment technique, that thought changes to "My mind says that I'm not good enough." Again, have a look at it. Remember that you're in control and that it's just a thought that's trying to get you 'hooked.' Be interested in it, as in: "Really, my mind says that I'm not good enough. What an interesting thought – but hey, it's not me. It's just my mind. I can see it trying to get me interested, but I'm going to stay as the observer of it. That way, I don't get hooked in."

The third example changes from: "I'M WORRIED THAT _____" to "My mind is worried that _____." Again you can be interested in that statement, as in: "Really? My mind says that? My mind does worry a lot. It doesn't really help me at all. Now that I can see that thought I'll let it drift away. I am an oak tree, and my thought is floating away into the clouds."

Notice what we're doing here. This technique of replacing "I" with "My mind" allows you to put some distance between your concept of 'I' and your mind. It gives you the perspective you need, and breaks the strong identification you may have with your beliefs.

If you want to change something in your life, you'll never do it by thinking negatively. Those negative patterns of thought actually rob you of your life force. So let's be clear that they're not YOU. They're just thoughts in your mind. Get used to seeing them that way, as robbers and thieves. Turn them into cartoon characters and see them gradually disappear when you simply acknowledge them.

Sometimes I sit down and write them all down on a piece of paper. That way I can have a good laugh at my mind! I can fill a page with thoughts that don't serve me: "My mind says... that I won't succeed... that I should worry... that she'll leave me... that I need to make sure that everyone likes me... that I shouldn't speak the truth... that I'm not attractive... that I shouldn't forgive her... that there isn't enough time... that I'll never have enough money." If you think you're the only one who struggles with your mind, think again. You're not alone. All of us have minds that try to disempower us at times.

It's easy to delude ourselves into this line of thinking: "Oh well, just think the opposite thought. Think positive!" Listen, if it was that easy, the world would be full of happy positive people! We desperately try to think positive instead of negative thoughts. But that means we're still the thinker! In effect we're giving the negative thoughts energy by resisting them. I prefer the technique of putting distance between us and our minds. When we don't attach to or fight with our thoughts they gradually lighten and leave because they're not who we are. They're just thoughts. When we let them go, they return to the consciousness that they came from. We'll look at all of that in a later chapter.

Once we have some space between us and any thought pattern or belief that makes us feel bad, we start to see them as entertainment! We don't put ourselves down for having them, as that only adds to even more negativity. Instead we simply notice all the commentaries, scripts and subplots that are running in our minds and we watch them the same way we watch the movies. After a while we get bored watching the same movies over and over again. We can have a good laugh at them. Finally the day comes when we change channels or switch the damn TV off!

Hopefully you've realized that this technique of dis-identifying from your mind is a very powerful step on your journey. Osho, one of my favorite teachers, has some strange images that have helped me with this dis-identifying. He says:

Try to be headless. Visualize yourself as headless; move headlessly. It sounds absurd, but it is one of the most important exercises. Try it, and then you will know. Walk and feel as if you have no head. In the beginning it will be only 'as if.' It will be very weird. But by and by you will settle down.

A few days of this and you will feel a tremendous silence, because it is the head that causes all the problems.

Another way of getting in touch with this non-attachment is to use a technique called inquiry. Ask yourself this very BIG question – "What survives in me if I stop thinking about it for five minutes?" Close your eyes, let the question come into your belly and feel into it. Take the five minutes. See what happens.

I hope that you understand how important it is to have your mind on neutral – open and receptive. Take a breath, settle down and let my words penetrate your belly. Yes, that's what I said – penetrate your belly – I'm glad you're awake! Seriously though, the center of your body is the belly, called Tantien in China, and Hara in Japan. It is the gravity center of the body. If you were a suitcase, we'd attach the handle to a point about an inch below your belly button and lift you up from there.

If you practice martial arts, you know what I'm talking about. When you're centered it's as if you have a different presence. You feel rooted and connected to the earth. It feels like you have such a deep inner anchor that nothing can pull you away or push you over. Try it now. Close your eyes and put your hand just below your belly button. Now begin to breathe into that area. Imagine that 'YOU' are 'there.' As you breathe in, focus on drawing energy into your center. When you breathe out, focus on moving the energy out to the extremities of your body. It might feel a bit strange at first. After a few minutes, you will start to feel from down there. Now imagine someone talking to you and that the words are coming in through the belly center. You'll find that you won't react as quickly when you 'hear' the words in your belly. It gives you that vital gap so that you can respond rather than react.

We're used to listening to the little 'I' voice in our heads but the bigger 'I' is all of you. The hara or tantien is the center of 'all of you.' Listen from this part of you and get used to this deeper awareness. Then you will transcend the conflicts of head and heart, thought and feeling, mind and emotions. You will start to respond to life from your center, rather than react from your head, full of all its nonsense.

As we develop awareness we learn to stop the patterns of thinking we have normalized: the holding on, holding back, holding in. The deflecting and pretending. The avoidance. We notice how often we are replaying the past or worrying about the future. We see our minds fighting with the present and we choose to stop. Finally we are taking the reins. It feels good!

Exercise

Here's a little exercise to see where you're at. You wake up one day with a certain amount of energy – your energy bank. During the day ahead you will use up a lot of that energy – your energy withdrawals. How well you use it and how much you have left depends on what deposits you make and how conscious you are of the withdrawals.

For the purposes of this exercise, let's focus purely on the mental aspect of your existence. Let's see how Angela rated herself in a workshop of mine in 2011 – she was very honest in answering all the questions on her assessment form.

Q. 1: How much of your time do you spend thinking or talking about what happened in the past?

Angela – "About 25%."

Q. 2: How much of your time do you spend thinking or talking about the future in a negative way?

Angela – "I worry a lot, so maybe another 25%."

Adding those two together, we see that 50% of Angela's time was spent thinking about the past or the future, leaving only 50% to deal with the present.

Q. 3: When you are focusing on the present (i.e. what's actually happening in your life right now) how much of that time is spent thinking that it should be different, or thinking about it in any negative way?

Angela – "I'd say 75%."

So while Angela has about half of her mental energy left to deal with the present, she wastes 75% of that. In her assessment, we find that she's left with only one-quarter of one-half (12.5%) of her mental energy in thinking thoughts that use her energy wisely. The remaining 87.5% of her thinking is a complete waste of her mental energy.

Now do the exercise yourself.

What was your final figure?

Chapter 4

The Victim, the Child and the Truth

Be yourself, because everybody else has been taken.
– Oscar Wilde

I remember making an appointment with a doctor in the early stages of my awakening. I hadn't been feeling well. I couldn't point to what exactly it was but my energy had felt low for about six months. When I started to speak in energy terms the doctor's eyes glazed over. He didn't want to hear about my lack of focus, my brain fog or my diet. All he wanted to do was diagnose me with a specific problem. After eight minutes he seemed to have decided that I was depressed and so he duly dispatched me with a prescription for antidepressants.

I felt very frustrated. I knew that I wasn't depressed. If anything, I was suffering from a very common malaise in society – NSU – or Non-Specific Unhappiness. I guess that most of us periodically suffer from this – a lack of motivation and energy, loss of enjoyment, pessimism, irritability, insomnia, and either a lack of appetite or overindulgence in food. I decided I didn't want to hand my happiness over to an ever-increasing dosage of pills. So, I persevered with searching for an answer that did not include medication and was eventually led to a woman in south Dublin. She was a fully qualified doctor and a homeopath. I phoned, made an appointment and arrived at a well-to-do detached house in the suburbs of Dublin a week later. There was no 'Surgery' sign outside so I simply rang the doorbell. It was answered by a middle-aged woman with a lovely smile. "You must be Eoin," she said. "Come on in."

This was different. What, no receptionist? No sterile waiting room piled high with magazines extolling the latest diet, telling us we're not thin enough and that we need more beauty products? No radio blaring loudly? No automated ticket or announcement system? This house exuded a peace and calm that I wasn't used to, and I felt myself softening as I walked behind her. She sat me down in a comfortable armchair and handed me a glass of water. "So what's the problem, Eoin?" She had this very disconcerting habit of actually being interested in me and gazing directly at me, as if she was looking for something. She also listened very well and she never interrupted. I wasn't used to this level of attention from anyone, never mind a doctor. I felt exposed, constantly shifting in my seat.

"So, it's been a tough time for you?"

"Yes, I suppose so, though it hasn't been that bad. Lots of people have it tough."

"Really? How are you with sympathy?" Holy moly, what a question! Nobody had ever asked me that before.

"What do you need right now in your life?"

My heart felt as if it was being gently invited to open, and I could feel myself wanting to cry – but real men don't do that, do they? I also wanted to run out the door, but real men don't do that either, do they? So I stayed and swallowed my tears. That's what real men do, isn't it?

An hour and twenty minutes later I left this wonderful woman, feeling much lighter in myself. Three days later I telephoned her.

"I can't stop crying today," I said.

"Have you been taking the homoeopathic remedies I gave you?"

"Yes," I said, "but I can't stop the tears. It's been three hours now, almost nonstop. I feel like I'm collapsing."

"It's perfect," she said, "you'll be through this in two more days."

She was absolutely right. Within a week I was feeling optimistic and hopeful about my future. Thankfully she never once mentioned medication, beta-blockers or antidepressants. They weren't what I needed at that time.

I have had clients coming to me who were prescribed antidepressants for many years and became addicted to them, when what they probably needed at the time was the kind of doctor I had just experienced. Someone who had the patience to listen and be compassionate, without needing to rush into a diagnosis and write a solution straightaway. But doctors are constrained by a system that needs us to need a tablet – otherwise the pharmaceutical industry loses its billions. It's a lose-lose situation for us, the gullible consumer.

If I ever feel unwell these days I have a look at my lifestyle. Is there anything that could be at least partly responsible for this, in my diet? In my environment? In my thinking? Is there anything I am holding in, holding back, holding onto, holding out on? Is there anything I'm not saying? Do I need a break for a day or a weekend? Do I need a massage to release tension in my body? Do I need to punch some pillows and scream to release some frustration or anger? Is there anything I need to talk about with my partner/lover?

In Ireland – and, I suspect in most other countries – our doctor's appointments are frantic, rushed and timed for 10 to 12 minutes maximum. Our health system is not a holistic system where the connections between mind and body are recognized. It seems almost incredible that we have not moved beyond the traditional model, though I suspect that the pharmaceutical industry has a lot of sway in ensuring that we don't empower people to solve their problems (effects) by going to the real solution (cause). The doling out of tablets and prescriptions are all fixated on the effect. We don't want to look at the deeper cause, whether we're eating badly, stressing unnecessarily, thinking or drinking too much. "Give me relief, give me a tablet. Then I won't have to change my habits or behavior." Sad, but true.

The structures of our health systems seem to buy into this victim mentality. As M. Scott Peck noticed in his book *The Road Less Travelled*, people don't want a cure. They just want relief. When the victim mentality is hardwired into your psyche, you don't even think of the possibility of self-empowerment. The victim in us wants someone else to take responsibility. In her work on archetypes, Caroline Myss talks a lot about the child and the victim, two of the archetypes that we need to transcend on our journey. It's comfortable to play the victim rather than step into an authentic power. We prefer to moan and blame rather than take the reins of our own lives. Many of us who walk around in adult bodies are also children, psychologically. We want someone to take care of us, while we keep on abusing our bodies and abdicating our personal responsibility.

When I was in the hospital I saw a very visceral representation of that. The man opposite me was on a ventilator for emphysema. Every two hours he would drag himself out of bed, wheezing badly. He would disappear for about fifteen minutes, telling the nurses that he was off to the toilet. When he came back each time he was reeking of cigarette smoke. What can you do when someone is deliberating causing their illness? What can you do when someone is in total denial? My attitude is simple. If you want help with your illness, then surely you have some responsibility in ensuring that you get well. That may mean that you've got to commit to some changes in your life.

Some charities and religiously-inspired initiatives can also hinder personal responsibility while thinking that they're actually helping. I read recently that a new charity has been set up in Belfast city to help drunks to sober up late at night. The charity runs a Mobile Alcohol Recovery Center, complete with beds and showers! While some politicians praised the initiative, there's something not quite right about it. A society that normalizes the idea that it's OK to binge drink and then spends taxpayers' money and charitable donations helping you to get 'undrunk' is a little insane. I prefer the solution that the city of Orleans in France came up with recently. If you get so drunk that you need assistance, you will be fined to cover the transport costs of an ambulance and the police and hospital services you may need. Makes sense to me! Accountability rocks!

Sometimes we need the truth rather than a pill or a remedy, even though we won't like it. Some of our beliefs around welfare and benefits need to be challenged. We have so many people unemployed yet there's so much that needs to be done. Why can't we mobilize all of that potential? The idea that a government should pay you to do nothing, subsidize some of your bills and also provide you with housing and other benefits doesn't make any sense to me. Not long-term. It doesn't empower people at all. In fact, it does the opposite. Too many benefits can strengthen the child and victim archetypes, so that we end up believing we need to be looked after, even if we're not sick. I've been in difficult circumstances myself a few times in my life, and I can tell you that I needed and appreciated a HAND-UP at times. But, a HAND-OUT would not have been good for me.

A handout would have meant that I could stay stuck, down in the hole I had landed in. If you're down in the hole you don't have to take any real responsibility (child archetype) and you can complain and moan all the time too (victim archetype). Too many handouts can be a powerful demotivator too. It's easy to normalize being down in the hole and believe that you're powerless. When someone offers a hand-up you don't want it. The hole becomes your comfort zone.

A gentleman knocks on his son's door.

"Jaime," he says, "wake up!"

Jaime answers, "I don't want to get up, Papa."

The father shouts, "Get up, you have to go to school."

Jaime says, "I don't want to go to school."

"Why not?" asks the father.

"Three reasons," says Jaime. "First, because it's so dull; second, the kids tease me; and third, I hate school."

Father, "Well, I am going to give you three reasons why you must go to school.

First, because it is your duty.

Second, because you are forty-five years old, and

third, because you are the headmaster."

– Anthony De Mello, *Awareness*

Wake up, wake up! You've grown up. You're too big to be asleep. Wake up! Stop playing with your toys. Most people tell you they want to get out of kindergarten, but don't believe them. Don't believe them! All they want you to do is to mend their broken toys. "Give me back my wife. Give me back my job. Give me back my money. Give me back my reputation, my success." This is what they want; they want their toys replaced. That's all. Even the best psychologist will tell you that, that people don't really want to be cured. What they want is relief; a cure is painful.

When you wake up, you begin to move away from the various tribes you belong to. It's a necessary part of the process. Most of us enjoy belonging to a tribe of some sort. Religious tribes, each with their own set of beliefs. The tribe of single parent, which has its own set of beliefs too. The middle-income tribe. The tribe that believes they're superior because they're highly intelligent. We belong to many different tribes, whether that's the tribe of teenager, the "recently became a parent tribe," the Corporate Person Tribe, the Hard-Done-By Tribe, the Hippy Spiritual Seeker Tribe, the Law of Attraction Tribe and even the Men-are-useless Tribe! While it's nice to feel a kinship with a particular tribe, remember that every tribe needs individuals who accept and agree with the tribal norms and beliefs. Otherwise there is no tribe.

If you're a man, you grew up with particular tribal beliefs, depending on the culture and society of your childhood years.

Same for a woman. Tribal beliefs can be anything that your 'tribe' believed and normalized. It could be that you have tribal beliefs about what it means to be a man and how a woman should relate to a man. You may have a tribal belief about what strength is and whether emotions should be expressed. You may unconsciously believe certain things about people with money, about what it means to be spiritual and whether sex can be deliciously fulfilling. And so on, ad infinitum.

By the way, when you discard a set of tribal beliefs, don't make the mistake I did. Whenever I discarded any old set of beliefs, I seemed to dive straight into taking on a new set of beliefs! I jumped from Catholic to Christian to Agnostic to New Ager! I guess it's a bit like the rebellious teenager in us that at some point said, "No" to the authority of the parent – but we never realized that we had jumped straight into another tribe because of our need to belong. Suddenly we believed everything that the tribe of teenager believed, what was the best music, how stupid our parents were and so on. We hadn't grown into ourselves fully. We were still reacting rather than finding our true individuality.

Many of us still don't get it. We don't see that our relationship to money and abundance may still be governed by our early tribal beliefs. There's an old belief that said that money was in some way sinful. Poverty and having less was in some way 'better' than having more. Many of us still have a sneaking suspicion that we can't be spiritual and have money. So, if you're, let's say, a 'good person' AND you happen to be wealthy, you'll find yourself giving to charity and doing good works – all to alleviate the subconscious guilt you have around money. There's nothing wrong with that but you need to be aware of the under-lying motivation.

There's a story told of the disciple who went to the Master, and said to him:

"I have come to offer you my service."

The Master said –

"If you dropped the 'I,' service would certainly follow. You could give all your goods to feed the poor and your body to be burnt and not have love at all. Keep your goods – and drop the 'I.' Don't burn your body; burn the ego. Love will instantly arise."

A few thousand years ago, somebody said that money is the root of all evil. That statement needs to be understood in its depth. It's the attachment to the money that's the problem, and, on a deeper level, it's the attachment to anything that causes the problems. Once you're attached to something, you don't want to let it go. Even a tribal belief.

As we move into this Brave New World and begin to individuate, we need to recognize that we carry some of the tribal legacies of the past with us. When we burst out of whatever set of beliefs had authority over us we often experience the pendulum effect, where we swing too far to the other side. We break from rules and structure, only to find ourselves without any sense of boundaries or containment at all. We can be a bit like the trippy hippies of the 60s except we're more wheatgrass and angels than cannabis and free love, although they're still around too. Nothing wrong with either, but we need the balance. In the breaking free from one tribe, notice if you're now part of another tribe. For instance, in opening up to the feminine it's important not to reject the masculine.

If we truly want to individuate, we do need to open up. To our need for love, support and nurture. To guidance, intuition and a deeper knowing. That's the feminine aspect of individuation. When you're opened up like this, you often get what we call an intuitive hit, where you simply know what needs to happen. You need to act on those hits. This is where the masculine aspect comes in to take action, based on the deeper knowing of the feminine. Another way of looking at it is that the head is now in service to the heart. You will know what needs to be done. "What do I need to do? Where will I go? What will I say?" These are the types of questions that guide us deeper. Listen carefully to the answers and take the required action. Often you won't know why. You won't know how it will all work out. But, as you work with this deeper knowing and develop your 'trust muscle,' a mysterious intelligence begins to reveal itself to you. Your mind goes quiet, your feminine intuition awakens, and your powerful masculine aspect takes direct action, busting through any remaining fear. Your sense of being separate dissolves, and you feel purposeful and connected.

Remember, though, that the world that we live in doesn't want you to be free to make your own decisions. It doesn't want empowered people who refuse to be victims. It actually needs you to be a slave to the consumer culture. It doesn't want fearless people either, because they're dangerous. Think Jesus, John Kennedy, Gandhi, Martin Luther King. They all challenged the old paradigms of the world in their time. In our time, right now, we live in a world paradigm that is based on fear. This foundational fear has spawned greed, anxiety, defensiveness and control. This paradigm needs to crack and crumble and be rebuilt. How? One person at a time. That's how the new world will emerge – one person at a time. The old in us, me and you, needs to crack and crumble and be rebuilt too.

First, we need to admit to ourselves that our own foundations are based on fear too. We need to be honest with ourselves. We need to admit our own greed, our own defensiveness, our own anxiety and need for control.

All spiritual traditions seem to agree that we have lost our way and that we are all on a journey back to God, wholeness, call it what you like. The shamanic tradition focuses on journeying into other realms to reclaim those bits of ourselves that we have lost. The healing traditions focus on liberating us – from our hurt, wounds and pain. The meditative traditions focus on sitting with our suffering and allowing it to subtly transform. The Christian traditions focus on redemption from our ignorance. The holistic model emphasizes moving towards wholeness, integrating and embodying the whole of who we are. This emphasis on integration rings very true to me because it discounts the need for salvation through some external God, whether that's Jesus, Allah, Shiva, or whatever you're having. It takes the emphasis off the brokenness, off the woundedness, off the pain.

That's important because our egos like us to keep 'scratching the itch' or, to put it another way, 'picking at the wound.' I've worked with clients who had been seeing their therapist for years, scratching the same wound over and over again. Telling your story over and over doesn't work. It simply ensures that you stay stuck in victim mode. So why continue telling the story? One of my favorite questions to ask clients is, "Who are you without your story?" Most of us are stumped by that question, because we've never inquired that deeply into ourselves.

If you're a healer or counsellor or psychotherapist, it's also very easy to become delusional, and end up with the infamous Messiah complex, where you really believe that everyone needs fixing – by you! That balance between humility, ignorance and arrogance is quite tricky. It's very easy to acquire a Spiritual Ego! You are here first and foremost to integrate and heal yourself, to see all your own blind spots, your own fears and your own arrogance. Whenever I get a whiff of that Spiritual Ego in myself I remember the famous Zen saying: "Chop wood, Carry water."

While I agree that we are all broken in one sense, our acknowledgment and acceptance of that is what makes us truly human. Our willingness to admit our vulnerability and weaknesses is, paradoxically, our strength. It frees us up. The amazing power of Jesus came from his courage, his willingness to drop all defenses, to keep his ego in check ("get thee behind me") and to be vulnerable. What did he hold onto? Zero. Zilch. Nada. Nothing. That's not how most of us think about power, is it? We think of power as holding onto lots of things, having control over assets, money and people. But that's not power. That's control. That's greed. That's the world of ego.

This deeper power is nothing to do with what you have, or how you control the circumstances of your life. It's the power to be yourself just as you are in each moment. It's the power to be naked and vulnerable, foolish and wise. It's the power to do what you want and need to, to say what you want and need to, to be clear about what you desire, without demand. It's the power to be authentic, to establish your boundaries, to speak your truth, to be open about your needs, to be fulfilled and happy.

It took me a few years to trust the vulnerability of this type of power. It nurtures us and allows room for our weaknesses as well as our strengths. It allows room for others too, along with their weaknesses and strengths. It allows us to ask for support when needed. Many men are fearful of this more feminine type of power which is more inclusive and interested in love and connection, rather than confrontation and power struggle.

Listening to and acting on this mysterious intelligence, this deeper knowing, will have a huge effect on your life, as I discovered in 2009 when I decided that I wanted to take a holistic holiday for myself. Every year a brochure would arrive in the post from a holistic resort called Skyros in Greece, and I would thumb through it eagerly. Every year for the previous three years I was disappointed, because nothing seemed to suit me. There were weeklong holidays for people interested in any yoga, creative writing, dancing, healing and so on, but nothing seemed to suit my calendar and my needs.

This time I decided to widen my search. Surely there were other holistic centers in Europe that were offering similar holidays? I googled for a while and came across a center in Italy, which was called The Hill That Breathes. I must say that I liked the name, which was based on the fact that the hill supported 40,000 trees, all breathing pure oxygen into the air. I began to search through the various weeklong options for May, June and July, reading the short blurb for each one. I was immediately drawn to a week entitled "The Fool on the Hill." It wasn't really a holiday, though. It was a weeklong retreat with a man called the Barefoot Doctor. Wiki says he (Stephen Russell is his real name) is a practitioner and teacher of Taoism, its medicine, philosophy, meditation practices and martial arts and manifesting system, or wu wei. I had never heard of this man and didn't know his work, but something deep in me said, "You've got to go there. That's where you need to be!"

My logical mind rebelled and said, "You don't even know this guy. I thought you wanted a holiday, not a deep retreat." By this stage in my development I had learned that sometimes I needed to ignore my logical mind and respond to the inner nudge, which in this case was quite insistent. And so I booked my week in Italy and flew off in late May to enjoy the Tuscan sunshine. When I arrived I discovered that over twenty of us had flown in from different parts of the world and that there was one other person from Ireland. That person was Jenny Grainger from Belfast, and meeting her was a pivotal point in my life. To cut a romantic story short, we are now life partners, moving deeper and deeper into surrender, truth and love. I will expand on relationship and love in a later chapter.

As you can see from my story, acting on your deeper knowing is incredibly important. It's very important to be able to discern what's right for you, and what's not, particularly when you're looking for a retreat or teacher to work with. Remember that the self-help world has become an industry and has a lot of clever marketing behind it. Those clever marketers know that we can be suckers, especially when we're low and vulnerable. They've hyped up a world-wide obsession with self-help and personal development, so it's now a huge industry. Beware! While some of it is good, some of it is downright dangerous. You too can be suckered, like an ex-business colleague of mine who paid over

€6,000 for a week with a well-known 'guru' in the self-help world. When she arrived at the venue she found that 'he' wouldn't be there in person. One of his accredited trainers was presenting the full week. When she looked again at the marketing material, she saw that it was cleverly misleading but stopped short of outright lies. Anyhow, she was there and it was too late. The brochures, competitions for free tickets, videos and promos all promised you everything you wanted. Your whole life would be changed in seven days.

Naturally, she felt betrayed and let down, which is not a good start to a week that promised you so much. She made her feelings known to the organizers, and joined the throngs. Less than twenty-four hours later, in front of the whole audience, this 'guru's' substitute pressurized her into revealing how she felt. She said she felt betrayed by the organization. He couldn't accept that, as it would have undermined him and the organization. So he told her that she simply had an authority "problem" and grilled her relentlessly. She felt trapped. As over 300 pairs of eyes bored into her she finally collapsed and admitted that she had been sexually abused by her father.

Little did this facilitator know that he had just replicated the same power and control dynamic that her father had exercised over her as a young girl. I think the term 'Parallel Processing' may describe what went on in that workshop. It's defined by some as "the unaware replaying, within the helping relationship, of a pattern of relationship brought from outside."

This woman had a complete meltdown that day and went home immediately. She took a full two years to recover psychologically and emotionally. She never got her money back either. If you're new to the journey please be discerning about who you work with. If it seems too good to be true, it probably is! If you have any doubts, back off. If there's an amazing amount of hype, be careful. The best people to work with are people who come highly recommended, not by marketers, but by friends or colleagues whose opinion you value. As you grow more into yourself you will be able to discern the difference between the real and the genuine, between the authentic and the hype.

Many of you have gone to college and worked hard for three or four years to get your degree. If you got a high grade, you might have gone on to sit a Master's degree, investing another two years of your life. So five years later, after much blood, sweat and tears, you can say you have a MSc in Applied Technology, or a Master's in Philosophy, or one of thousands of other possibilities. Here's the thing – they all require bags of commitment and dedication. The term Master implies that you've invested a lot of time and effort at your chosen specialism. Yet here in the self-help industry, they're handing out Master's Degrees like sweets at a fairground!

I googled Reiki Master yesterday. How many years does it take to be a Master of Reiki? Oops, sorry, it doesn't take years. In the Reiki Academy in London it takes two weekends and a five-day workshop – nine days in total – to become a Master. Really? Who are we fooling with the term "Master"? Wait, it gets worse! I've just seen that you can get Reiki Level I, II and Master Certification online for less than $50. You take an online course and hey presto, you're a Master too! With this you get three manuals plus your distance attunements for all three levels plus your certificate from your Instructor/Master once you successfully complete this course. Once you're a Master, then you can train others to be Masters. You are now empowered to attune others. Really? Fifty dollars and an online course makes you a Master of Energy, empowered to attune others! Says who? Who empowers you? What qualifies you for empowerment?

When someone says to you, "I'm a Reiki Master," it's supposed to sound impressive. But what does it mean? It may simply mean that he or she has paid money to train for a few days with someone who trained with someone else over a few days – and so on. You get the picture. All of a sudden we have an explosion of 'Masters' – Reiki Masters, IET Masters, Tantric Masters, Seventh Level Ascended Violet Flame Masters of the Black Star. OK, I made the last one up! But we do have to laugh at ourselves if we believe we're Masters of something after a few weekends, or now after doing an online course! Who are we fooling?

Real Masters don't need to tell you that they're Masters. You'll know just be being around them. A real Master is someone who has spent a lifetime getting to know themselves in all their darkness and all their light, without needing to identify with either aspect of the opposite poles that live inside us all. Real Masters are ordinary people, like you, like me, humbled by the immensity of the mystery we are living. They radiate a presence, not a personality. There's a world of difference.

Chapter 5

A Near Death

A near-death experience (NDE) is a personal experience associated with impending death, encompassing multiple possible sensations including detachment from the body, feelings of levitation, total serenity, security, warmth, the experience of absolute dissolution, and the presence of a light.
– Wikipedia

It was Christmas Eve and I had met some friends at a local bar. I remember being very sensible that night and having one pint of lager and one of lemonade, knowing that I had to drive across Dublin later on. My girlfriend and I left the bar at about 11pm, and I started up the motorbike. Twenty-five minutes later I'm travelling at about 45 miles per hour, rounding a gentle bend in the road. Right there, in the middle of the road, there's a car, side-on to me. It looks like it's not moving, though I can see a driver in it. I've only got a second – literally!

Once that second passes I'm going to T-Bone that car which, for some unknown reason, is doing a U-turn in the middle of a bend. The reason turns out to be that the driver is drunk. He stopped for fish and chips, came back out to his car and decided to do a U-turn. My bad luck!

A very surreal experience followed, as time slowed down, or at least it seemed that way. It was probably my first experience of being fully present to the moment because, in half a second or so, I made three key decisions.

1   The road is wet, so don't brake too hard because the bike will go down and we'll both slide into the car and break something.

2   Straighten the bike right now so that we don't go in sideways and break our legs.

3   Stand up now, as tall as you can, on the foot pegs. As you hit the car, Deirdre (my girlfriend) will shoot up over your back and land in the road somewhere. With luck, you will go right over the car too.

As it turns out, I didn't go right over it. One of my legs caught in the handlebars, and so my head smashed into the car, full-on. I passed out. I remember some voices and then seeing my body on the ground in the middle of the road. Floating above yourself is a very strange experience but at the time it seemed quite natural. Then the voices and the scene dissolved, and I could hear and see nothing. But it wasn't dark at all; quite the opposite. I felt as if I was being gently transported somewhere, as all around me opened up into a swirling vortex of purples and whites and violets. I felt myself being drawn further and further into this beautiful mishmash of soft sky and warm clouds, all wrapped around me. I felt very safe even though I didn't have a body anymore.

The colors around me gradually got brighter and brighter, and all traces of purples and violets began to disappear. Everything opened up into a vast expanse of pure white just in front of me, and I was fully cocooned and held within this new universe. I felt incredible joy, the deepest peace imaginable and the sure knowing that I was almost home. I felt like I belonged here even though I had no sense of my physicality at all. Everything was welcoming and supporting. Every second was like the softest caress imaginable, even though time had ceased to exist. I melted into IT. I merged with IT. I was a part of IT. IT was me. I was IT. All was White. All was Love. I was HOME.

BAM! It all changed in a millisecond! I went from being limitless, pure and white, to being constricted inside a 5'7" masculine body which was laying on a stretcher in the ambulance as it roared towards the hospital. A giant of a man was straddling me, his fists rhythmically pounding my chest. An oxygen mask was fitted to my mouth and I began to breathe again. I clearly remember thinking: "I want to go back. Damn it. I want to go back. I wanted to stay a bit longer!"

I had glimpsed something ineffable, something beyond the limited "I" that we all talk so freely about. When we say, "I'm worried," what we really mean is, "My mind is thinking a thought that doesn't feel too good, and I feel the result of that thought in my body." But we're not our minds, or our bodies, or our emotions. So, what are we?

My near-death experience opened me up to a deep knowing, that I AM the one experiencing everything. I AM the one experiencing my body. I AM the one experiencing my thoughts. I AM the one feeling the sensations. I AM the one flowing with my creativity, feeling my emotions and trusting my intuition. I AM the one experiencing myself writing these words. I AM awareness. I AM consciousness. From this place I can watch everything coming and going. My body. My thoughts. My emotions. Your body. The world. I can sit right back into this dimension of awareness, or consciousness, and see everything that's happening out there – but 'I' am here. Now. Present.

Yes, I know that it's difficult to really understand what I'm saying – because it's not 'of the mind.' My hope is that this book helps you to taste what it's like to transcend your limited view of yourself and to say, "Hello" to your intrinsic essence. May you come home to yourself as deeply as I have.

Let's rewind a little, to March 1993. At that time, if you were to have a peek at my life, it looked pretty cool. I had a family, a house, a mortgage, two cars and all the usual stuff that goes along with a reasonably successful suburban lifestyle. But I wasn't fulfilled. Something was missing. Something was stirring inside me, a restless searching feeling. I'm not sure if I was looking for God or looking for Me or searching for a Deeper

Happiness, or were they all the same thing in a funny kind of way? After a few false starts I found myself, a few years later, attending my first ever retreat. It was a four-day event with about thirty other men. I was in my mid-thirties by now, and yes, I was nervous. Who wouldn't be? It was way outside my comfort zone, revealing my thoughts and feelings to complete strangers!

That was the first time I allowed myself to think some big questions. Who am I? What's life all about? Am I really successful – or am I fooling myself? What is success anyway? Who measures it? Why can't I love me? Something began to open in me when I allowed myself to feel into the questions, without looking for answers straightaway. These questions allowed me to soften some of the hardness around my heart, an outer shell that I had accumulated over many years. That shell had protected me from feeling deeply – and I suppose it was necessary at different points in my life. Somewhere in my past I had taken on the belief that emotions like sadness, abandonment, frustration and anger were not to be felt. If anything, they were to be buried. So that's what I had done. I had buried them for years. On that retreat I asked myself a very BIG QUESTION: "Where did I bury them?" I pondered that one for a while until I realized that they were buried in ME. Somewhere deep inside ME was all the sadness, all the anger and frustration and all of the unfelt emotions. They were all in the basement somewhere. They had never died. They were buried alive!

That realization woke me up. I saw many basements opening up over those few days. I witnessed other men speaking truth, exorcising demons and shedding layers of their own past. As the days progressed I noticed how easy it was for some men to speak openly about themselves. Some spoke of terrible thoughts they had. Some spoke of how much they hated themselves and how useless they felt. Some spoke of terrible things they had done. At the beginning of the retreat I would have judged them. Now I was beginning to understand. I saw that we were all lost in different ways, even those who appeared to have 'made it.' As I listened more I made the mental leap from judgment to understanding. Allied to that I made the leap from SYMPATHY FOR to EMPATHY WITH them. Empathy is the ability to FEEL WITH others, without telling them it's OK, or jumping in to try and fix it because you can't how accept raw it makes you feel.

The whole experience somehow 'gave me permission' to open up too. Even though it was a challenge for me to allow myself to cry in front of others, it was a release too. Everything in my 'basement' was stirring, wanting to be freed. At one point I wept openly for almost half an hour. (Kleenex did well that day!) My body had begun to allow what was buried to come to the surface and I gradually released some of what had been stored inside. As the weekend developed I saw something else clearly. I saw that when we open up and reveal our true selves, we become more beautiful. We become more authentic.

Courage starts with showing up and letting ourselves be seen.
– Brené Brown, *Daring Greatly*

We all need to wake up to the fact that hiding just doesn't cut it anymore. We need to be honest with ourselves. Why? Because, deep down, we all know that it hurts to hide ourselves away, behind the pretense and the masks. Most of us spend years and years propping up a self-image that we want others to see. It damages our self-esteem because what we're really saying is, "The real me is not loveable, so I'll show you a pretend me. I'll show you the 'Me' I think you want to see. Hopefully you'll love the self-image I show you."

The problem is that IT'S NOT YOU. IT'S AN IMAGE OF YOU. This image has no depth and no substance. It's totally dependent on what others think and what the world thinks. It has no connection to the authentic you. My own self-image didn't want me to admit that I had messed up in life and that I had needs and desires too. It saw vulnerability as weakness. It didn't want me to speak openly with others because that meant that it would crumble. But I knew that it was time for me to face up to the truth. I had generated my own self-image which needed my energy to keep it propped up. A few years later I realized that having any self-image didn't feel useful to me, whether a positive one or a negative one. Any image was a distortion. It was a pretense. I didn't need an image anymore. I needed ME, but where was 'ME'?

It was very challenging for me to admit to myself that I felt very lost and that I didn't know the way forward. It's not something most of us men are comfortable with, but it felt somehow right. I allowed myself to trust that deeper knowing.

After those four days I came home on a high. "Buzzing!" is the best term I can find to describe my state. The buzz lasted a few days and then disappeared, but something had changed. A seed had been sown. It was as if I had been given something priceless, a glimpse into the possibility of freedom, the freedom to be me! So I decided to nurture this new possibility. I remember thinking: "Is this what life is supposed to be about, a journey into being free? Free of our minds, free of the relentless pressure of our self-image, needing to measure up to something indefinable?"

Whereas before the seed had been planted in my head (aka beliefs about Life, Love, God and the Universe), this time the seed had reached the fertile ground of my heart. I DESIRED the deeper dimensions. I DESIRED peace, love and understanding. I DESIRED trust, intimacy and surrender into the arms of something indefinably beautiful. I realized that I couldn't integrate these desires while I was full of fear, anxiety, distrust, judgment and resentment. So I prayed that those deeper desires would manifest. In modern speak, I 'put the intention out there.'

I began to see myself as being in the 'classroom of life.' Everything that came along in my life had a lesson that needed to be understood with my head AND taken deep into my heart

AND integrated into the fabric of my being. So I started to use my life situations as 'teachers' for this newfound way of being. Why? Because time and again, life was showing me the ways in which I wasn't free. Life turns out to be a great teacher if you're willing to listen. Here's two simple examples.

FACT: I had always been drawn to needy types. I liked being around them, helping and guiding them.

REALIZATION: I needed to 'do good' and be seen as a 'good person' because, in truth, I didn't feel good about me. There were bits of me that I wasn't ready to face up to. So I had to be doing something to feel loved and appreciated by others. When you look at it that way it's pretty ridiculous! Remember the newborn baby? It doesn't have to 'do' anything to deserve love. Being is enough. So I had to look at my tendency to bolster my own self-esteem by helping the needy types and appearing to be a good guy. That way I didn't have to admit to myself how needy I was, that I craved love and understanding too!

FACT: I seemed to attract strong forceful personalities, though I didn't like them at all.

REALIZATION: My mind kept judging them as bullies, arrogant and self-centered. The whole thing was backwards! What was really going on was that I had work to do on embracing my anger and my lack of power in the face of people like that. There was nothing 'wrong' with them at all. They were just showing me where I was disconnected from my own strength.

Life turns out to be the most amazing teacher you'll ever come across. Fast-forward a few years, and my marriage was slowly crumbling. The belief I grew up with was that marriage was for life. Therefore this slow breakdown shouldn't be happening. I had always imagined that we would be together in a traditional marriage with a few kids, a nice house in the suburbs and barbecues in the summer. Mow the lawn every now and then, and take the kids to the playground. Buy their first bicycles and teach them how to ride. Watch them grow into teenagers, all moody and all-knowing! Watch them explore their boundaries. Watch them experiment with alcohol, sex and drugs. Watch them learn how far they could go. Watch them rebel against me when I laid down any rules or set any boundaries. Love them for that rebelliousness while still clipping their wings a little. Watch them grow into adults and have their own kids as we became doting grandparents.

But it wasn't to be. I wasn't happy. Although I looked fine on the outside, I was stressed, unmotivated and generally down in the dumps a lot of the time. It's that syndrome again – NSU or 'Non-Specific Unhappiness.' I was now in my late thirties, things were difficult, and I was "hanging on in quiet desperation." Why? Because letting go would somehow mean that I was a failure. I found it hard to let go of this life I had built, partly because I had been married for many years. Even though our thoughts about how we should parent, what was important, and how life could be lived were very different, we stayed together. I suppose that I hadn't the guts to leave because I imagined that my marriage would last. I thought we could hold it all together even though the foundations were crumbling. It took years and years, like the slow crumbling of an ancient edifice. The outside of the marriage still looked OK, unless you got up close. There were cracks in the walls and the roof had caved in. Although the walls were standing, there was no real life inside. We had drifted apart. It happens.

I had also discovered an emptiness deep inside myself and I filled it with different things. I tried overworking, pushing for success in the business world. It didn't make me happy. I tried alcohol, which just gave me temporary relief, and the next day, made the empty feeling even worse. I even tried zero alcohol for a few years but that made me very self-righteous and brittle. I tried religion too, starting with the Jehovah's Witnesses for a while. They seem so sure of themselves and I wanted some of that! We all need something to hang onto when we're going through doubt and despair. I didn't like the chaos and uncertainty at all.

For a while, then, I took comfort in this easily defined Jehovah's Witnesses' God who had a few simple rules to follow. If I believed that I was an unworthy sinner and kept the rules, then I could be redeemed by this God. It took me a while to realize why I was settling for this God of Conditional Love, who was very similar to the God of my Catholic upbringing, full of fear and judgment and righteousness. He had a large finger that pointed to your sins, every day and every night. You had to visit with him on a regular basis and ask forgiveness. If you did this, you were part of his family and you were saved. If you weren't part of God's family, you were doomed, just like the rest of humanity.

After many years flirting with the Jehovah's Witnesses and more evangelical Christianity, I began to see how self-important I had become. My thoughts were full of self-righteousness and comparison, and I was unable to look at myself or others without judgment. When you're brainwashed into believing that you're 'good' then it follows that others who aren't brainwashed are 'bad.' Most people I met in these religions had disowned their shadow, and genuinely believed that they were good. Some went so far as to believe that they were the chosen ones! To borrow a phrase from *The Blues Brothers* movie, they were "on a mission from God."

I really wanted to believe that too but somehow I knew that their God wasn't for me. I wanted a warm, moist, comfortable God, one that could inhabit me – not a cold and distant figure that relied on fear to force me to be 'good.' Mind you, it's easy to believe in a God that doesn't require you to think for yourself, a

God that only asks you for a small bit of your time every week and, of course, a financial contribution! But slowly and inexorably, I turned away from any way of thinking that was based on fear.

My relationship with my wife had also turned from sweet to neutral to sour, slowly fermenting into distaste and resentment as our marriage gradually collapsed in on itself. I knew that we were not good for each other anymore, but I held on. Our paths were obviously different, but I still held on! At this stage I thought my marriage was on its last legs, but they turned out to be remarkably resilient legs! Finally I got emotionally involved with a younger woman for a few months (which seems like the classic midlife crisis) and even though it didn't escalate into a full-blown affair, I had begun to look outside of the marriage. Something was missing, and I wanted to find it. It's hard for me to remember what I was like back then, but thankfully I wrote a diary, parts of which have survived:

Diary – February 2001

I'm sitting at my wife's vanity mirror staring at myself. My home, my kids, my wife, they've taken up so much space in my life until now, what will I do? We've done so many things together. We've dreamed things together. We still own things together. "Not anymore," says that bloody voice inside my head.

I look around the bedroom. Is it her bed now? Is it mine? Who owns what? What will happen? Where will I live? What will happen to the kids? The questions keep coming, relentless, powerful, unstoppable. I feel helpless. I should know the answers, shouldn't I? I don't.

I glance in the mirror again, seeing the wispy grey hairs around my right nipple and the darkening line descending from my belly button into the red boxers. Will any woman ever look at me again, at my age? I mean, 43? I'm no spring chicken, right? Will I ever look at myself again and be proud of what I see? Right now I just feel sick at the sight of me, because my marriage is all but over. Nothing feels relevant anymore, and those damn lyrics kept going round and round in my head... "You may find yourself in a beautiful house with a beautiful wife... You may ask yourself, well, how did I get here?" The question seems to have got stuck in the vinyl groove inside my brain: "How did I get here?" "HOW THE HELL DID I GET HERE?"

The question stayed there, gouging deep furrows in my mind. How did I get here? My right hand fingers the wedding ring, turning it over and over again. It seems to belong to another world, one that I had gotten used to living in. Now, though, I feel as if I am leaving that world and heading for an unknown planet. If I never come back, would anybody care? Maybe that's the best thing. Just give up, Eoin. Exit stage left. Leave the earth. Now. Take a load of pills, lie on the bed and never get up again. Drive the car at speed into a brick wall. Anything at all will do it – there are lots of ways.

"For fuck's sake!"

A strong voice. An angry voice.

"Stop it," says the voice, "you're driving yourself crazy."

"Am I?"

"Yes," says the angry voice, "now get dressed and do something, anything." I've heard that voice before. It's the immensely practical one, based on common sense. But there are other voices too, all competing for attention. "I couldn't be bothered," says another voice. "Fuck off," says another. "You're a waste of space," says another. "It's true, you're a waste of space, your wife agrees."

I can easily drift into hopelessness. I just want to float around in space, jettisoning bits of my life that don't work, and hover on the outskirts for a while. That's a whole lot easier than having to deal with this mess. It's partly – no, mainly –

my mess.

But at least I can clean up some of it, somehow. "That's what a real man does," says another voice. I grab on to that one. There's no point in giving up – I'm not a wimp, even though I have plenty of voices inside which disagree. I have made many changes in my life which needed courage. I grab more evidence for myself. Hey, I've provided for four kids while self-employed for fifteen years. That's no mean feat.

I stand up, grab my shirt and trousers and walk out of the bedroom. This will be a strange day, but hey, I'm a survivor!

When my marriage and family finally broke up, it awakened a whirlwind of emotions in me. I felt so lost, scared and confused that I was forced to open my heart to others. I'm glad I did because up to then I had focused on 'soldiering on' or 'putting a brave face on it,' all those phrases we use to represent denial of what's actually happening. As I opened up to my unfelt emotions, I was led into deep healing, introspection and spiritual growth. During the years ahead I danced with life, recognizing my inner resistance to joy, shedding layer after layer each year. I took advanced healing courses, learned new communication skills, and trained as a transpersonal counsellor. I sashayed over hot coals at dusk, to the sound of a shaman's drumbeat. I trained to be a public speaker. I meditated. I got up close and very personal in my Tantric explorations.

Just like Shrek, I was discovering that we are like onions! I shed layers and layers of 'stuff' – and sure enough I began to touch into an authentic self which felt very different to the 'old me.' Yes, my friends and family thought I was nuts, and they still do! When you step outside tribal belief systems and social norms you begin to rock the boat. The world doesn't 'get' you anymore, because you're not gettable! You don't do drama. You don't buy into the manipulation and power games within most relation-ships. You don't buy into the way the world works, or rather the way the world doesn't work! You've totally redefined who you are and that's a very beautiful thing to do. You're finally free to be you. It's like you've finally come home, which is exactly how I felt during my near-death experience.

You see, we now have tons and tons of knowledge at our fingertips, thanks to Google. But, and here's the catch, knowledge isn't what we need. If you look at the professions who have dedicated years of their lives to knowledge about health and well-being, you'll see this truth for yourself. I'm appalled at the number of doctors, psychologists and counsellors who are stressed, anxious and obviously unhealthy. What use is all your knowledge when you're desperately unhappy?

We have enough knowledge. What we need to do is to start applying what we know, to put it into action. It's easy to stand on the sidelines and spectate rather than get involved in the game of life. It's easy to know that you're in the wrong job or wrong relationship or that you need to speak up more. What's more challenging is to do something about it. And yet we still buy more books and attend more seminars because we desperately want to believe in these gurus and their products. We want to talk the talk just like they do. We're not that keen to 'walk the walk.'

However, walking the walk is the most exhilarating thing you'll ever do in your life. It will push you to the edges of who you think you are. It will awaken all your fears too. It's also why you're here, on this planet, at this time. You're here to drop all those crazy ideas you have about yourself. You're here to move beyond your current experience. You're here to explore your edges and to experience joy. You're here to find a depth of peace that nobody can take away. You're here to understand the incredible power of vulnerability and defenselessness. You're here to stop pouring your energy into maintaining the past, worrying about the future and trying to control life so that it doesn't bother you. Give it up!

You're here to surrender to the wisdom that wants to be

birthed through you. All you have to do is cooperate with life and what it throws at you. Life will show you where your edges are, where your limited thinking is, where you resist, defend and deny. Watch it all, open into it all and grow beyond it all.

Exercise

Your layers and strategies of protection have many names. They are variously called programming, rationalization, pretense, deflection, negativity, acting out, blame, fear, closing down, projection, denial, holding back, holding in, intellectualization – and many more.

Name one way that you pretend.

_____

What does it show about you? Be curious about it.

_____

_____

_____

Name one way that you judge.

_____

What does it show about you? Be curious about it.

_____

_____

_____

Name one trigger that gets you really annoyed.

_____

What does it show about you? Be curious about it.

_____

_____

_____

Chapter 6

It Is What It Is

He has lost his grip on reality.
The only way I can help him is to show him
the difference between what's real – and what's in his mind.
– From the movie *A Beautiful Mind*

I always use a chair to demonstrate this teaching to a class. I take a simple white chair and say, "This is a white chair. Do you all agree?" They usually laugh, because it's a silly question! Everyone knows it's a white chair and so they nod their heads, saying, "Yes, we agree." Simple. "It is what it is" – a chair, a white chair.

"That's wonderful," I say. "We have managed to see it for what it is. We don't need it to change in any way. There's no need to push it away. There's no need to grasp for it. There is no attachment to wanting it to be different. There's no judgment or criticism being passed on. Our energy towards it is balanced and neutral. OK, so far."

Then I change that by saying something like, "I wish it was brown," or "That chair should have a higher back," or "I don't like that chair" or perhaps even stronger, "That chair shouldn't be allowed to exist!" Now my mind is involved in wanting the chair to be different. But it's not different. Nothing has changed and the chair is still the same. All my wishing it was different hasn't made an ounce of difference to the chair, yet I've used up some of my precious energy in a futile war which I cannot win. Of course, it's a ridiculous situation, who wants a chair to be different? But the concept is valid because this is what we do – with people, with ourselves, with situations, even with our thoughts and desires. We fight with them, we resist them. We tell ourselves, "He should be more understanding" or "She should be different." We also tell ourselves, "I should be fitter" or "I shouldn't drink so much." Again we're fighting with reality. This mental resistance is a waste of our reservoir of energy, and it begins to constrict the natural acceptance of what is. We start to form patterns of resistance that become habitual inside, and so our outward behavior follows suit. As Anthony De Mello said in his wonderful book *Awareness*, we become "puppets." Something happens, and we react a certain way. The same thing happens five years later, and we're still reacting the same way! Who's in charge of our lives?

We can easily become puppets, reacting this way and that to what life brings us, without any inner awareness of our ability to respond rather than react. We've forgotten that we're creating our own misery and our own stress and suffering, because we're blind to our reactive habits, unconscious beliefs and internal assumptions. The mind creates its own peculiar logic and beliefs, hardwires these into our psyche, and our 'normal' behavior patterns are established. If you watch closely, you'll find that the vast majority of what you do is conditioned and reactive, rather than responsive or creative.

So it's a really good practice to learn to pull back to 'IT IS WHAT IT IS.' In other words, we don't tell ourselves that it should be different, or that the person in front of us should be different, or that life should be different, or even that we should be different. Why? Because it isn't different – IT IS WHAT IT IS. If I had a magic wand, I'd have that tattooed inside our foreheads so that we'd all remember to stop fighting reality. We can never win that battle!

Here's a simple example. You're stuck in traffic, the car is hardly moving and you're going to be delayed. For most of us, a situation like this leads to a feeling of stress or anxiety, because we want the situation to be different. However, if we spot that tattoo inside our foreheads, we can remind to ourselves of IT IS

WHAT IT IS. It's a traffic jam. I can accept that or I can fight with it. If I accept it then I am at peace. If I fight with it I won't win, but I will waste precious energy and give further weight to my usual reactive patterns. Added to that I will cause myself stress, frustration and possibly even anger.

It's always your choice. You can resist reality or you can accept it. Acceptance of 'WHAT IS' is the only intelligent response to life. (By the way, that doesn't mean we condone everything. We'll have a look at that later.) Resistance of WHAT IS could be classified as some form of insanity, but we can't say that, can we, because we all do it. We seem to think that it's quite normal to waste all our energy thinking we know how others should run their lives, and yet be desperately unhappy. Perhaps it's more 'sane' to take the emphasis off what's happening out there, and focus on our internal world, because that's the only thing we have power over. Unfortunately it can become quite normal for us to bitch about life, to blame others, to tell ourselves it's hopeless and to hold on tightly to self-important opinions and beliefs. We're like the spectators at a football match who get very agitated about what's happening on the pitch. It easier to look at the game than to look at our reactions to the game. Life is happening all the time, just like the football match, but we're not playing. We're not participating. We're simply reacting, over and over again. When we don't look at our reactions, they 'become' us. These reactions use up our energy, often leaving us feeling exhausted and powerless. We've no energy FOR life itself because we've wasted all our energy reacting TO life!

Let's take this 'IT IS WHAT IT IS' teaching deeper into your psyche. I want you to imagine you've just been down to your local tattoo artist and you now have this tattooed on the INSIDE of your forehead. "IT IS WHAT IT IS." Walk around with it for a while. It's a really powerful way to look at the world. Why? Because it's TRUTH. Seeing through this new lens will open up a huge reservoir of energy that you've been wasting by feeding your habitual reactions TO life. You haven't been cooperating WITH life, have you? (Don't worry about it, we're all the same. It's not personal – it is what it is!)

So let's take our story a stage further. Imagine that the traffic jam eventually frees up and you get to your workplace on time. You're busy at work, deep in the middle of something you're enjoying. Your manager comes across and asks you to drop everything to help out with somebody else's project. If you're like me, you'd probably react to this in a negative way, but you can't say what you think – because it's your boss. Now there're two opposing forces at work within you, the desire to speak and the need to keep your mouth shut, in case you lose your job!

The real trick in these cases is to put some distance between 'the inside' you and whatever's going on 'outside you.' If you don't, you will be triggered into a reaction, not a response. You need to look at the new tattoo you've just inscribed on the inside of your forehead. "IT IS WHAT IT IS." When you do that, it will set off a new train of thought, which is exactly what we want. You may see that reality is simply happening and that you have a choice how you want to be with reality. You don't have to resist it. If you're more advanced you may see that your boss simply had a thought and communicated that thought by speaking some words. You slow down enough to see that some sound vibrations travelled from his voice box across the space and landed at your eardrums. That's all. It is what it is. You don't have to react.

It's up to you, and there's no right or wrong here. Remember the idea is that you don't waste energy by fighting with what is. That means that you let the words pass through, and then decide what your response is, rather than react. Response and reaction are very different. A response might be, "I'd love to help out, but it will be at least half an hour before I finish what I'm doing. If I drop everything I'm working on now, I will be letting some customers down. Are you OK with that?"

The added bonus in taking this energetic step back is that now you're in charge of how you want to respond. You're not reacting at all. It feels very empowering to NOT react in your normal programmed habitual way. Sometimes the easiest way to do this is so simple it eludes us. All we need to do is take a breath and remember the tattoo on the inside of our foreheads. "IT IS WHAT IT IS." When you're not in reactive mode, you may be able to respond in a way that surprises you. For the moment, you're not a puppet!

There is a huge difference between living a reactive life and living a creative life. The middle space between reactive and creative is acceptance, and the statement "it is what it is" moves you from reactive behavior into that middle space of acceptance. Once you can stay in that middle space of acceptance, you can move to the next step, which is to recognize that it's not all of you that's reacting. It's just a part of you. It's important to develop the awareness that a part of you has been activated. But it's not you. It's just a part of you. 'You' are the one watching this triggered part of you that wants to engage. This part of you wants to feed off the drama and the resulting inner turmoil. If you don't see it clearly, it will fire up unconsciously and continue the momentum of your habitual energy patterns, whether that's resentment, frustration, withdrawal – or simply blowing your top!

These parts of us that lie dormant until triggered like this are aspects of ourselves that are being brought to consciousness. We need to bring love and acceptance to the reactions themselves rather than saying, "I shouldn't react like that," or "I'm not a very conscious human being," or "That's not a very loving response." The statement "IT IS WHAT IT IS" is also very useful here. It enables us to accept our internal reaction to whatever is happening externally, without judgment. As the wonderful novelist Anais Nin put it, "We don't see things as they are, we see them as we are."

That's OK though. It's very important not to judge yourself when you notice your own triggers and reactions. As you go deeper into discovering what's at work within you, you will find a voice constantly saying things like this to you: "You shouldn't be stressed." "You shouldn't be angry." "You shouldn't be anxious."

This voice wants to find something wrong with either the external situation/person, or with you! That's its job, to find something wrong. As you begin to practice deeper and deeper acceptance of 'what is' you will notice that this negative aspect of your mind will get very busy, trying to convince you that there is something wrong, somewhere, anywhere! If your negative mind can't find something wrong, then it begins to freak out, because it knows that without something to oppose, it will die. Naturally enough, it does not want that, and so it will do everything in its power to bring up situations that will reinforce your habitual reactions and negativity. It's good to notice that this critical voice is purely a reactive voice because it's scared. You'll see that it gets very scared of your newfound acceptance of reality. You will probably notice reactive thoughts like: "But you can't accept that," or "If you accept that, you're just a wimp," or "Don't be stupid, anxiety is normal. Just look at the number of people suffering from it" – and so on. It will do anything to justify its position as the dominant voice in your mind.

Let's remind ourselves that the reason we're constantly affirming "IT IS WHAT IT IS," and the reason that it works, is because it simply is the Truth. As we were told over 2,000 years ago by the man called Jesus, the Truth will set you free. "I AM THAT I AM" is a personalized version of "IT IS WHAT IT IS." They are both Truth. They can't be argued with. These are very simple but profound teachings. If you can keep reminding yourself of statements that resonate with TRUTH, you will set yourself free. Yes, it is a process and yes, you'll mess it up sometimes. Remember that you, like me, are a 'work-in-progress.' We just keep going. We just keep fine-tuning. What begins to happen is that you notice more and more how easily you get 'hooked' into some form of drama or resistance or negativity. The Buddhists use the word "Shenpa" to describe the 'hook' energy that triggers us into our habitual tendencies. It helps us to understand that something out there is throwing us a hook, with some form of bait that we're familiar with. Our job is very simply to notice the hook and the bait, and then to ignore it. Eventually the 'fisherman' will go away.

I hope that, by now, you're constantly aware of that reminder I asked you to tattoo on the inside of your forehead – "IT IS WHAT IT IS." The other version of it, that's also true, is this: "IT WAS WHAT IT WAS." Arguing with the past – 'what was' – or telling yourself it should have been different is NOT intelligent. It's madness, because, again, you'll never win. Telling yourself, "He should have... known better," or "She shouldn't have done that," doesn't change what happened. It never will, so stop arguing with the past. Things happened. Accept it, and move on. If you can't accept it, get help and support, and tease it out. Yes, it may take a while, but ultimately, you need to get your mind and body to move on. Remember that none of us were surrounded by enlightened beings all the time, so we all have our wounds, hurts and pain. None of us were born to enlightened parents, and my own children, who are all adults now, would heartily agree to that statement!

Deepening your awareness of what's actually going on in your inner world will help you to see that some of your energy patterns don't serve you. You begin to see where you are stuck, how you are hooked, and what is really holding you back from a life of pure aliveness and well-being. As you begin to notice and not get hooked into the old patterns, you free up your true nature of love, joy and expansion, and your energy bank grows. You begin to maximize the amount of energy at your disposal. In plain speak, you feel more alive, you look healthier and you begin to enjoy this strange and wonderful life.

By the way, you're not on your own here. There are many

others who struggle with the circumstances of their lives – and yet are afraid to leave the familiar territory they know. I remember days when I felt like Shrek. I didn't want to leave MY swamp.

But we do don't we. We need to leave the familiar and embark on the journey. As you peel back the layers you will be amazed at what you didn't know about yourself. Hopefully you'll have the courage to embrace everything you find inside, and one day, realize that what the sages had been saying over the centuries is true. All is well. It's my favorite affirmation, those three simple words. ALL IS WELL. That doesn't mean that we condone everything that is happening. We simply recognize that there's a deeper intelligence at work and that, despite the suffering and chaos in the world, we're evolving towards something better. Each one of us is called to do what we can do. That may mean you take action by modelling to your children how to love without conditions. It may mean you move away from something that's not good for you. It may mean you start a new business. It may mean you learn to look after your body in a more loving way, or take your first real holiday, or start teaching, healing or helping in some way. Everyone has their own path.

Looking back now I am thankful to all the 'ordinary' people I met along the way, especially those I couldn't bear to be around, those that I fell out of love with, those that I blamed and those that I didn't speak my truth to. They were my teachers. They revealed to me the parts of myself that I had rejected, or, in psychological language, the parts of me that I had 'put into shadow.' Learning to accept and ultimately love those parts of me didn't happen overnight, but gradually, in the midst of all these challenges and stresses and turbulent emotions, I began to sense the seeds of who I really was.

It's not any different for you. There's a journey to be undertaken – and you've already begun. Most of the material for your foundations is available to you right now, in the 'stuff' of your life. That's how spiritual alchemy works – we take what's actually presenting in our lives, and we work with it until the truth reveals itself to us. But you'll never taste the truth until you drop your opinions and projections, and see life as 'IT IS WHAT IT IS.'

Write down an example of how you fight with, or resist, reality.

_____

_____

_____

How will you feel if you stop fighting/resisting?

_____

_____

_____

What might happen when you do stop?

_____

_____

_____

Take one more example of where you resist what is. Write it down.

_____

_____

_____

How will you feel if you stop fighting/resisting?

_____

_____

_____

What might happen when you do stop?

_____

_____

_____

Chapter 7

Just For Today

Today's the day I've been waiting for
Tomorrow won't come after all
Yesterday is so far away
And today is the only day.
– *Today's the Day*, Pink

BEEP-BEEP-BEEP. BEEP-BEEP-BEEP. WAKE UP! Your alarm is beeping. It's morning – again! The alarm beeps again, ten minutes later, and you realize that you'd hit the snooze button. Damn! So you crawl out of bed, shout for the kids to wake up, and jump into the shower. While you're in the shower you're thinking of everything you need to get done today. By the time you're washed, you're already stressed. A quick makeover in front of the mirror, and then you're into the kitchen. The news tells you that three hundred jobs have been lost locally, a train has careered off a siding, and a terrorist has been shot dead as he tried to set off his suicide vest. The weather forecast is for more rain for the next five days, and there's gridlock on the motorway you use to get to work. It's 8:15am and already you're frazzled! The world has programmed your mood, because you didn't take the time to set it for yourself. Sound familiar?

Some of you have alarms that are deliberately obnoxious, while others stick with a 'relatively unpleasant' sound – like the noise a large truck makes when it's reversing! Ouch! What a way to start your day! That's your first mistake, being rudely jolted awake by a discordant or harsh sound. It sets your mind off on its usual negative rant, whatever that is for you. Mine used to be, "Oh, for God's sake, already? It feels like I have just fallen asleep. Do I really have to get up?" Just to be clear, that didn't come out of my mouth every morning, but it was my inner commentary! My default morning used to start with me getting up as late as possible – and then all hell would break loose. Not a great way to start a new day. If I have to set an alarm these days, I use a gentle ringtone or piece of music that fades in over a period of time. It helps.

Sometimes I ask my clients, "Do you shower in the morning?" Most of them squint their eyes and look at me strangely, to work out if I'm serious or joking! I hold my best poker face until they blurt out, "Of course, at least, well, almost every morning." I then put on my 'really serious' face, and I innocently ask, "Why? Why do you shower every morning?" The answer is invariably some variation of… "to clean off yesterday's dirt… to feel fresher." "OK," I say, "so you have a physical shower almost every morning, to clean your physical body. Great. Do you have a psychological cleanup, scrubbing off yesterday's negativity?" I know, it's a strange question, but it's useful. We're more likely to remember it when it's a strange question. It took me a while to realize that I was carrying all of yesterday's psychological dirt and emotional baggage into every new day. I never made the time to STOP and set myself up for the day. I just rushed headlong into it, unconsciously carrying all my yesterdays with me.

So it makes complete sense to me to take an extra five minutes each morning to take charge of how I want to be for that day. If you don't do it, the world will set your mood for you. We are bombarded daily with negativity, sensationalism, drama, traffic jams, deadlines and so on – and these will all hook you back in to your 'normal mode' – unless you have programmed your day by setting your intention and sticking to it. Yes, it will take a little time. A new habit takes about twenty-one days to integrate into your life so that it becomes your norm, and this little habit only takes five minutes. You can spare five minutes even if you have to get up earlier. Try it for twenty-one days and see what happens. If you're like most people, you'll love it for two reasons.

One, because it only takes five minutes, and two, because it works! Finally, you're taking charge of how you want to experience life.

You can commit to doing anything for a day. All the twelve-step programs are based on this simple philosophy. They have a JUST FOR TODAY card, which is often read out at twelve-step meetings. I've changed the emphasis of this to focusing on how I want to be for a day. I've been setting my Daily Intention for many years now, and while I miss a few (because I'm a human, not a robot) it's my most regular practice. Today's Intention was: "Just for today, I am receptive." Setting a Daily Intention is a very powerful practice, and my clients tell me that it's very effective for them. We know that it really works. Set an Intention. One day at a time. Simple. Effective. Intelligent.

The best way to integrate this into your life is to get a routine that works for you each morning. If you've convinced yourself that you haven't got the time then it's even more important for you. Make the time! Have your physical shower and then take five minutes to have a psychological shower too. It's not that difficult. It becomes a habit, just like your physical shower. It sets you up for the day and gives you back the reins of your life.

I'm guessing that you want to be master of your own destiny rather than a puppet of the world. It's a no-brainer, isn't it? So, tomorrow you get up five minutes earlier. You stretch and breathe a few deep breaths as you settle into your shower, imagining that the water is cleansing you of any leftover baggage from yesterday. You allow yourself to let go of any stories in your mind that don't serve you any longer. After you step out and dry yourself, you follow that with your Intention Setting practice. Five minutes is all you need. Light a candle. Close the door. Tell the kids it's your "special time." Tell the dog to get lost! Just make it YOUR time, and build this positive habit that will transform your life.

So, what is it – Setting an Intention? It's different to setting a goal, which might be making a call, changing your job or running a marathon. A goal can feel quite 'hard' until you begin to ask yourself questions like, "Why do I want to do this?" or "What's the essence of this for me?" That will point you towards the Intention. The Intention is more about: "How do I want to BE today?" What you're doing is programming your Inner World because, if you don't, the world will do it for you! Here's a few of my favorite intentions:

Just for today, I am strong.
Just for today, I am calm.
Just for today, I believe in myself a little more.
Just for today, I am confident.
Just for today, I am receptive.

Most of the words that come to me describe an emotional state, as in: "How do I want to BE?" So, ask yourself that question each morning: "How do I want to BE?" When you get the right words, close your eyes and breathe in the energy of your Intention Statement.

Here's a few words that may resonate with you. Just for today I am:

accepting – accomplished – affectionate – appreciative – authentic – balanced – calm – centered – clear – communicative – compassionate – confident – connected – considerate – constructive – cooperative – courageous – creative – curious – dynamic – eager – easy-going – enthusiastic – flexible – focused – free – friendly – frisky – fulfilled – gentle – graceful – gracious – grounded – happy – harmonious – healthy – helpful – honest – hopeful – humble – innocent – inspired – joyous – kind – light-hearted – mature – motivated – observant – open-minded – optimistic – passionate – patient – peaceful – playful – present – productive – receptive –

reflective – relaxed – resourceful – respectful – responsible – serene – sincere – spirited – spontaneous – still – strong – supportive – tender – thankful – trusting.

So you breathe in, for instance, "I am calm," and you let yourself imagine what it's like to feel calm. If you can remember times in the past where you were very calm, bring them to mind. Perhaps you attended a meditation or mindfulness class once, or it could be an experience you had in a church, or a mosque, or walking on the seashore. If you can't bring a particular experience to mind, simply let your imagination do the work. Remember that your body doesn't know the difference between a real experience and an imagined one. Ramp up that imagination! You need to move through each of your senses to amplify the experience, and then we'll finish with what's called a psycho-neural anchor.

To recap, you've focused on the Intention/Feeling you've picked for the day ahead. We've picked 'calm' as our example here. Now you're watching yourself experiencing the state in your imagination. This is your visual sense. See yourself calmly walking along the seashore, for instance. Next, let yourself hear whatever is conducive to the experience. This is your auditory sense. It may be birdsong or the sound of the sea gently caressing the seashore. Find something auditory that works for you. Amplify both the visual and the auditory, and when you're ready, move into the olfactory sense, smell. Pick a smell that reminds you of being calm. It may be incense or a particular essential oil, or a particular fragrance from an old memory. It could even be the perfume your favorite auntie wore, or the smell of your grandfather's pipe when he smoked. Now you have three senses engaged: sight, sound and smell. Let yourself move more deeply into feeling it kinesthetically. What's it like to see yourself calm, to smell calming smells and to hear calming sounds? What does all that awaken in your body? Feel it all. Amplify it even more, and just as you are reaching the peak, you are ready to anchor the whole experience with what is called a mudra.

'Mudras' are hand positions used in Buddhism and in yoga, often in conjunction with the breath (pranayama). While a mudra is most beneficial when held for at least ten minutes, I have found that even a minute makes a difference. On your right or left hand (whichever feels more natural to you) simply touch the tip of the thumb to the tip of the middle finger. Now breathe in and associate that hand position with the strong feeling of calm you're experiencing. Say to yourself – "I am calm." Keep breathing deeply while touching your thumb and middle finger together. You have now created, in NLP terms, a psycho-neural anchor. This hand position is your anchor for the state of being you've decided is best for you today.

Later on, during the day, remember to touch your thumb and middle finger together, and recall the Intention you set earlier on that morning. Take a breath and remember the feeling of calm you anchored with the hand position. You can do this anywhere. You find yourself getting anxious and stressed just before an important meeting, so you pop in to the bathroom to freshen up. You take an extra minute to activate your anchor and you walk back out feeling refreshed and calm. If you're really stuck, you can do this with your hand in your pocket! The anchor recalls the feeling that you created earlier of being calm and centered. Use it whenever you need to.

That's pretty amazing when we allow ourselves to understand it. When you think an anxious thought, you experience anxiety. All you've done now is to go for a conscious thought. As you think yourself calm and imagine yourself calm, the energy of calm lands in your physical body as an experience that you can feel. Thought has created that experience. Thoughts always create, whether they're conscious or unconscious thoughts. Your level of consciousness determines how much creative power you have over the world that you are experiencing right now. It's also true that your level of unconsciousness determines how much reactive energy you waste over and over again. It's as if the world, in all its fear and drama, is sucking you dry. So setting a morning intention is like saying to the world – "Hey, you know what? I'm done with thinking the same crappy thoughts over and over again. From today on, I'M IN CHARGE!" It's akin to a boat dropping anchor in a stormy sea. Everything begins to settle and stabilize even though there may be chaos all around you.

I remember setting a regular morning intention of "Just for today, I am at peace" while minding my partner's 82-year-old father for a few weeks down in the Andalusian hills of Spain a few years ago. He was in the advanced stages of dementia, which meant that he often didn't know where he was, who I was, or whether he ate breakfast ten minutes ago. He would ask the same question over and over and repeat the same observation every few minutes. Usually it was something like, "Where am I?" or "There's not a cloud in the sky." Each time he'd say it as if it was a brand new question or observation. After a few days of this my mind began to react, firing up feelings of frustration and impatience. However, anytime I began to experience those feelings, I reminded myself of the intention I had consciously set: "Just for today, I am at peace." As I remembered my mudra, I touched my thumb and middle finger together and found that peaceful place within me. I dropped out of my head and into my heart, and found compassion for this old man. If I hadn't set my intention every day, I could have fed myself a starter of frustration, a main course of resentment, and a little bit of martyr for dessert! Setting a conscious intention each morning is a wonderful antidote to whatever is unconsciously operating in the background, robbing you of peace, joy and energy.

At the beginning of this new practice, give yourself some visual clues or reminders to remember your Intention during the day. After a few months you'll find yourself, on a regular basis, touching your thumb and middle finger together and taking a few breaths, as if it were completely normal. In other words, you will have finally taken charge of how you want to be. You are directing your energy according to your conscious INTENTION, and you're offering this energy out to the world. What does the world do? It mirrors it back to you.

We can see this quite clearly when we look at people's experience of life. Angry people live in an angry world. Judgmental people live in a harsh, judgmental world. Joyful people live in a joyful world. Peaceful people live in a peaceful world.

So the question is: Do you want to begin to live from the inside out, taking charge of your experience, or do you want to continue being a puppet, pulled this way and that by what's happening outside of you? It's always your choice, one day at a time.

Here are a few of my favorite Intentions:

Just for today, I believe in myself a little more.
Just for today, I allow myself to ask for support.
Just for today, my needs are valid. I will include my needs today.
Just for today, I listen deeply to my body.
(I remember all the times I did not listen to my body's messages – and I forgive myself completely. I did not have the awareness of the sacredness of the physical world and my place in it.)
Just for today, I communicate clearly.
(I remember all the times I did not voice my truth because of fear – and I forgive myself completely. I was not grounded enough in self-love to understand that fear is the absence of love.)
Just for today, I allow myself to have fun.
Just for today, I am compassionate, especially with myself.
(I remember all the times I acted without love – and I forgive myself completely. I was lost in the world of ego and did not know what real love was.)

Just for today, I am wise.

Just for today, I trust my intuition.

Just for today, I communicate openly and honestly.

Just for today, I trust that life is unfolding perfectly.

Just for today, I allow any resentment to leave me.

Just for today, I am open to wonderful surprises!

Just for today, I notice how often I compare myself.

Just for today, I drop all judgment of others.

Just for today, I speak from the heart.

Chapter 8

The Possibility Exists

Out there beyond the concepts of right and wrong, there is a field.
I'll meet you there.
– Rumi

This quote, translated from Persian, is attributed to Rumi, the thirteenth century Sufi poet. If Rumi had our current metaphysical language, he might have said that the field he was talking about was the quantum field where 'all things are possible.' If you think about it for a minute, it has to be true. Everything exists in some form of space. The tree grows into the space that's available to it. These words landed on a space that used to be a blank page. That piece of music that you love has to have background silence to exist in. That wonderful bit of percussion exists only because there's a deep underlying silence available to it, and each staccato beat drops into that subtle background space. Everything exists only because there's an accommodating space that allows it all.

Nothing can exist without the space to exist in. Space gives everything, including us, the freedom to be. This space is where all things come from and all things go to. Things come and go all the time. Everything is born and everything dies. Creation and destruction are happening all around us. Even the cells of your body are dying as you read this. New cells are taking their place. All things will die at some stage, including the planet we're standing on as it spins through the cosmos.

It's what Eckhart Tolle called form and formless. It's also called 'manifest' and 'unmanifest.' There's a limitless universe of unmanifest which is arriving every second into this manifest world that we see and experience. The things we see hear and touch are expressions of what has manifested from the unmanifest. What is a thing? It's anything we can describe. A book. A car. An elephant. A tree. A stone. A cactus. A thought. An idea.

It's important to realize this, because that space is available to everyone, including you. That space holds an infinite number of possibilities for your life. If we were thinking in terms of time, we could also call it the future. The future is what is coming into the present right now, in the same way as the manifest arrives and takes form as manifest. It's always arriving into the present. An idea pulls the future in and manifests the idea here on earth. Forty years ago, I couldn't have spoken into this little laptop and dictated these words. Two hundred years ago, if we'd even talked about planes and mobile phones, let alone a World Wide Web, we would have been dragged away to a sanatorium. If we'd talked about equality of the races and genders we would have been branded as crazy. Now, of course, all these things and ideas are commonplace and acceptable. We create, every day. We are always creating new things and new ideas. Ideas about equality, morality, gender, power, relationship, marriage and so on. The greatest gift we have been given, though, is the ability to create ourselves and our experience of life.

So I give you a challenge. The challenge is to open up to that possibility that you can create your outward experience of life by looking into your inner life. You've got to stop resisting this unstoppable force which actually wants you to cooperate with change. Open yourself up to the possibility of cooperating with the very Intelligence that underlies everything, the space that allows all things to be. As you do, you will realize that all possibilities do exist.

To understand and cooperate with this emerging consciousness means that we have to leave the two-dimensional world behind. Our minds have been programmed to think in dualistic terms – 'black and white' – 'gay and straight' – 'I'm right, you're wrong.' Now we're being invited to transcend that old style of thinking. In this new space where all things are possible, we are beginning to recognize the limitations of the mind that is divided against itself. We cannot go on fighting with ourselves 'inside' because that's what we create 'outside.' Our internal struggles will always be mirrored externally in poverty, war, inequality and greed.

In his wonderful book *Man's Search for Meaning*, Viktor Frankl tells us of his life in a German concentration camp in the 1940s. Some of his descriptions of what it was like for the prisoners are horrendous and beyond what most of us would be able to endure. Reading about his experience brought tears to my eyes as I read through the pages of his powerful story. In all honesty, I can't begin to understand what it was like for him. Amazingly, though, within the pain and suffering, Viktor Frankl had a profound awakening experience. He discovered something that was incredibly liberating. Even though his life situation was appalling, he recognized that the prison guards could not take one thing away from him – the power of choice. He was stripped of everything, but they couldn't take this one thing away. He put it like this: "Everything can be taken from a man but one thing: the last of the human freedoms – to choose one's attitude in any given set of circumstances, to choose one's own way."

His message struck me very powerfully. Choice. We all have it, yet how many of us exercise it? How often do you sit back into that space that allows all things, and then CHOOSE? How often do you remember that you have that space available to you, and that it's only you that decides how you will be, with your partner, with your boss, with that person who gets you to react the same way every time? You do decide, each time, consciously or unconsciously. If you decide consciously, you're in charge. If you decide unconsciously, something else is in charge.

Mostly, we are reacting to what life throws at us, so we're deciding unconsciously. But what if we could recognize that, in every moment, there's the possibility of choosing? Viktor Frankl understood that we need to consciously create a space in ourselves so that we're not triggered immediately. He said, "Between stimulus and response, there is a space. In that space is our power to choose our response. In our response lies our growth and our freedom."

This space between stimulus and response is also the space between the past and the future. The stimulus happened in the past (perhaps a half-second ago!) and the response will happen in the future (perhaps another half a second!). In between those two is the present, that space where possibility exists, potential can be tapped and manifestation can begin. I see it as a blank page where I get to write my script. The challenge most of us have is that we're not conscious enough to know that, in every second, there's a blank page awaiting our script.

I learned to train myself to remember that, in every situation, just like Viktor Frankl, all possibilities exist. If I can do it, so can you. Repeat these three words over and over again until they are burned into your subconscious. Take out the crayons or markers and spend half an hour drawing it out in different colors. Write it down as your password, or somewhere you'll see it every day. I have it on the outside of my kitchen cupboard. THE POSSIBILITY EXISTS. These three words will liberate you from reactivity, open you into possibility and fire up new creativity. All you have to do is to get your mind used to those three words. THE POSSIBILITY EXISTS is a very powerful statement because it's always true. If the possibility doesn't exist in your mind then it cannot happen. Remember that. Use those three words any time you find yourself reacting to what's happening or closing down in any way. Repeat them as often as you can, have fun with them and see how empowering they can be.

Here's a few examples. You're driving to an appointment. There's a traffic jam. You have to meet someone in fifteen minutes, and your mind begins to frame the thought that you'll be late. Damn! You hate being late. You can't even text the person you're meeting because you forgot your phone. Double damn! Your mind starts wondering what they will think of you. Then you remember to breathe, and to drop into that space between stimulus and response. The stimulus is already here – the traffic jam. The response is totally your choice once you remember the three words, and so you begin to try them out.

THE POSSIBILITY EXISTS… THAT I WON'T BE LATE. You like this possibility, but you're absolutely convinced you will be. So you try another one. THE POSSIBILITY EXISTS… THAT SHE'S DELAYED TOO AND WILL BE EVEN LATER. Hmmm. This one is possible. It feels a bit easier to go with this, because it's true. But what if she's not late? What if she's sitting there impatiently, waiting for me? So you try another one. THE POSSIBILITY EXISTS… THAT I WILL BE LATE, AND THAT I CAN BE OK WITH THAT. Result! You realize that, of course, it's possible for you to be OK with being late, so you open into it. You start to feel the possibility of being OK with it. Yes! Your breathing slows and you start to notice the car and the traffic in a different way. You try a few more, just for the fun of it. THE POSSIBILITY EXISTS… THAT I DON'T HAVE TO 'FIGHT' WITH WHAT'S ACTUALLY HAPPENING. Yes, that's a possibility. You begin to feel more in control of what you are thinking and feeling. Now that your mind is no longer fixated on fighting the situation, it moves towards a solution. THE POSSIBILITY EXISTS… THAT I COULD TURN ON SOME OF MY FAVORITE MUSIC AND RELAX. Job done! You have moved into creative mode, where YOU decide how you are with a situation.

There are so many possibilities that we can tune into in every moment, but we tend to be run by our unconscious reactions which are usually negative, stressful and possibly critical of ourselves. So I find it useful to keep those three words very close, using them as a remedy for reactive behavior and as an antidote to my Inner Critic. You know that critical voice inside, don't you? It's the one that's very strident and sure of itself. It shouts things like: "It'll never work out for you," or "You'll never be a writer!" or even "You're just a waste of space." When it starts a rant, I remind myself that all possibilities exist, and that all I have to do is to open my mind to that truth.

"It'll never work out for you" becomes... "The possibility exists that everything is working out perfectly."

"You'll never be a writer!" becomes... "The possibility exists that I am already a writer and you haven't caught up yet, because you're a voice from the past. The possibility exists that you're jealous!"

My favorite one for dealing with my Inner Critic is this: "The possibility exists that the only reason you exist is to show me what not to believe and how not to live. I love feeling into new possibilities. Thanks for pointing me in the right direction!" You'll find that the Critic doesn't like to be thanked! It's a powerful way to disarm it.

Here's a few more examples –

THE POSSIBILITY EXISTS... that I am learning to respond rather than react.
THE POSSIBILITY EXISTS... that no one is against me!
THE POSSIBILITY EXISTS... that my life is unfolding perfectly, without my mind needing to be so involved.
THE POSSIBILITY EXISTS... that I am enough just as I am.
THE POSSIBILITY EXISTS... that I am growing more and more confident each day.
THE POSSIBILITY EXISTS... that I have everything I need inside me!
THE POSSIBILITY EXISTS... that this day is a new beginning.
THE POSSIBILITY EXISTS... that I don't need to compare myself to anyone.
THE POSSIBILITY EXISTS... that whatever happens, I'll handle it!
THE POSSIBILITY EXISTS... that the more I relax the brighter my

future!

THE POSSIBILITY EXISTS... that I am exactly where I am supposed to be!

THE POSSIBILITY EXISTS... that every decision I make is the right one for me!

THE POSSIBILITY EXISTS... that my life will experience a dramatic shift as a result of reading this book and completing all the exercises!

THE POSSIBILITY EXISTS... that I don't need to know why she did that.

THE POSSIBILITY EXISTS... that I don't know how wonderful my future is looking already!

THE POSSIBILITY EXISTS... that all I have to do is believe in possibility and get excited by it!

Exercise

Fill in these sentences as if you really believed that anything was possible – which of course is true!

In five years' time I

_____

_____

_____

Never again will I

_____

_____

_____

Next month I will

_____

_____

_____

Each week for the next ten weeks I will

_____

_____

_____

I've learned how to

_____

_____

_____

The new thing I am trying out is

_____

_____

_____

The one thing I've stopped doing is

_____

_____

_____

Chapter 9

I Am Here Now

Past and future are in the mind only - I am now.
– Sri Nisargadatta Maharaj

The one Constant in life, according to the Buddha, is imperma-
nence. In other words, everything is changing all the time. Life is
all about the dance between what's coming and what's left
behind, and all of this happens in every moment. Even now the
past is leaving and the future is arriving – NOW! This 'NOW' is
strangely paradoxical because our minds can't understand it,
can't control it and can't put it in a box. It refuses to be conceptualized. Everything happens within the NOW, including all your
thoughts about it! Life cannot exist, and in fact only exists, in the
NOW – the two are inseparable! So, when we resist either the
NOW or the change within the NOW, we resist LIFE ITSELF –
and yes, it is that simple!

I saw a cool cartoon on Facebook today where the political
leader shouts out, "Who wants change?" Everyone in the
audience raises a hand enthusiastically. The next caption shows
him shouting out, "Who wants to change?" – and they all look
away! It's a bit like that for most of us. We want it, or him, or the
situation to change, but we don't want to change.

Life is always calling us into something new, in every
moment, every hour, every day. Resisting whatever change each
moment brings is, therefore, slightly insane – but we do it all the
time!

When we imagine all these moments strung out together, we
can see a time line where we put the past on the left, the future
on the right, and where we are NOW in the center. We imagine
ourselves walking along this timeline, taking steps towards the

future. But if that were the case then we would be moving away from the now, which is impossible. So what's really happening? It seems obvious to me that time itself is actually moving through the NOW, because the future is coming in, now, every second, now, and the past is leaving, now, every second, now... and so on. This is really important because it means that we can stop thinking of ourselves as moving towards our dreams, or achieving our goals. Our dreams are moving towards us! This is a new paradigm in which we simply open up to whatever is being brought into the NOW. In meditation practice we are asked to "stay with ourselves." In other words, we allow all the sounds to come to us. We allow all the sights to come to us. We stay in and with the moment. Everything comes to us.

Here's another way of looking at it. The words that I am writing NOW (October 2015) are NOW (whatever date YOU are in) being read by you. From my perspective, they have moved from my present to your future, whereas, from your perspective, they have moved from my past to your present. However, you and I both exist in the NOW (one of us is writing and the other is reading) – so I am therefore communicating with you across the dimension of time, which must therefore be contained WITHIN THE NOW. Yes, I know, it's a bit of a Mindbender!

When you move within the now, you stop grasping. You stop looking to the future for your fulfilment or to the past for your identity. You allow the NOW to inform you, always flowing with the deep realization that "the kingdom of God is within you." If you can begin to understand this, then you start to move into a space where there's no 'efforting.' There's no need to ruthlessly pursue your goals or to push for anything. As I said earlier, you begin to see that the future is moving towards you, and your consciousness fine-tunes what is being 'brought in.' This is where the real magic happens, so stay focused because it's really important to grasp this so that you can apply it.

When you think/dream/visualize something (let's say a new

job) you've already created it in the eternal present, at the level of thought. That much is easy. It hasn't arrived on planet earth yet, but at least the possibility has been created. There it is, up there somewhere in 'ThoughtLand.' For instance, the idea for this book was 'up there' for a long time. Lots of people dream about writing a book, but not everyone actually completes the process. Have you ever wondered why? Have you ever wondered if there's a 'roadmap' that could explain to you how dreams and ideas get converted into reality? We'll have a look at all of that later on in the book.

But for now, I want you to remember that you need to cooperate with this eternal moment, whatever it brings. You need to stop fighting reality, which manifests in many different ways in your life. Your job is to be OK with whatever arises, including being OK with yourself as a work-in-progress. You're not the finished product and you never will be. Even the universe is expanding in every moment! When you can look at life this way you realize that there is no endpoint and that there is nowhere to actually 'get to.' You can take a breath, stop TRYING to be good, stop TRYING to be enlightened, stop striving, stop efforting! Relax!

When you learn to be open and undefended against what's emerging in the moment, you experience life with great enthusiasm and aliveness. But most of us are not open and are undefended. We are constantly closing up against 'what's happening,' otherwise known as reality or 'life itself.' Remember that any moment is simply a space available to you to live in – right now. You can inhabit the moment in any way you want, but you need to understand that each moment is a microcosm of your life, and that each moment builds on and includes all the previous moments. All these MOMENTS produce the MOMENTUM of your life! Remember that every moment somehow includes every previous moment you have ever lived. I often compare the MOMENTUM in life to a snowball. It's got a certain mass, made up of all the previous moments of your life. If those moments were mainly negative, then there is negative momentum in your life. That momentum has energy, and it will live on for a while as you begin to change your life from the inside out. The most important thing for you is to stop ADDING to it. Don't make the snowball any bigger. Let it gradually melt and dissolve into nothing. Take your attention away from it and it will die. Start a new snowball with its own MOMENTUM. Add more and more moments of Acceptance. Add Moments of Gratitude. Moments of Honesty. Moments of Personal Responsibility. After a while your new snowball will have its own momentum. Keep feeding it with the good stuff, and be aware when the old snowball wants you to add more negativity or powerlessness or blame. Don't.

Moments are the building blocks of the future. They are also incredibly sacred, because each moment has immense depth, breadth and possibility within it. Unfortunately we have become very invested in using the moment simply as a way to get somewhere, so we pass through it with our eyes focused somewhere else, because we are overly identified with the grasping aspects of the mind. When we reduce time to a measure of our progress, we never taste the depth of the moment. Remember that our minds love to take a position on what's happening in the moment – and that position is usually deter-mined by the momentum of all the previous moments we've lived.

There are three basic ways in which the ego-mind takes a position on the moment, akin to the fight, flight or freeze responses that are invoked by fear. The fear-based response happens where the ego-mind sees what's happening in the moment as a threat in some way. When presented with something it doesn't like or feels threatened by, the ego-mind will do one of three things. It will:

1   Move away from what's happening in the moment.
2   Move towards what's happening in the moment.
3   Take a stand against what is happening in the moment.

When one of these responses is activated, we lose touch with the essence of the moment. We're not in the moment at all, we're in our heads.

Let's look at each one of these in order. When presented with something in the moment that it doesn't like, the ego-mind may "move away from" the situation. Let's say someone is saying something you don't want to hear. Your ego-mind will want to distance itself from the imagined threat to itself, so as to keep you safe. Of course that's an illusion, because there is no threat to the deeper you. However, the very act of the mind moving away from the moment means that you have energetically left your center. Your deep presence is not available to the situation because you're caught up in a mind story about what's happening. You'll feel it as a withdrawal from the situation, a closing down in some way. Let's take an example. You arrive at a dinner party only to find that your friend has cancelled and everyone around the table is a little loud, especially the man at the head of the table. His voice is loud and booming. This activates a negative psycho-neural anchor in you of times when your dad shouted at you when you were little. Your mind recalls that feeling of the scared child and so you energetically withdraw and close down to this man, in order to feel safe. Logically, of course, there's no threat in the moment. You're an adult, not a child. Your mind has created the imagined threat, based on a past impression, and so you withdraw and make yourself small and quiet. This withdrawal of energy will always happen when the external experience triggers something inside you that the mind doesn't like. That may be something you've done in the past or something you experienced. If the past experience is tinged with unresolved emotion – sadness, fear, guilt, shame – your mind will find a strategy to move away from it, into denial, secrecy, busyness, whatever.

The second strategy of the mind is to "move towards" something. When the external world brings something the ego-mind really likes, it's very easy to lose ourselves in the 'sweetness' of it or the idea of it. I remember being in an office full of women one day, and standing by the desk of one of the administrators. I was there as the company's business accountant, working on some information to present to the Board. I sat at this woman's desk, supposedly concentrating on the conversation we were having about the cash flow of the business. That's what we were talking about, but my mind had dived into her cleavage and was off in its own fantasy world! It happens to all men, whether we admit it or not!

Let's take another example. A woman has had a very insecure childhood, where she was abandoned by her father. Thirty-five years later she meets a lovely man who is everything she dreamed of. He makes her feel safe and secure. She loves these feelings so much that she doesn't realize she has moved away from her center, and she gets lost in the sweetness of this new relationship. She starts to become clingy when he doesn't phone every day. Eventually her very clinginess drives him away.

In this situation, the mind has found something it loved (a feeling of safety and security) which was activated by the external world when she met this man. This feeling was something she longed for as a child, so she gravitates towards it. It 'completes' her. When he doesn't phone, the feelings of the abandoned child are activated. She gets even more clingy, desperately wanting this feeling. She doesn't realize that, internally, she is moving away from the feeling of abandonment, because she doesn't like it, and towards the feeling of security. She will always do this in relationships until she learns to sit with her own feelings of abandonment, without grasping for the opposite feeling over and over again.

What we're looking for is the ability to enjoy the sweetness in each moment, without leaving our own center. I am not saying that we shouldn't enjoy the sweetness – quite the opposite! But the sweetness can take control of you too. We can disappear INTO anything – the sweetness of new relationships, or mind-altering drugs, or the sweetness of being wealthy. What happens for most people is that while the 'sweetness' is in their lives, the ego-mind is satiated. They're happy. But when the sweetness leaves or disappears then they find themselves suffering because they feel they have lost something. Their sense of self was heavily invested in the thing that gave them the sweetness. Men have jumped off bridges when they lost all their money. Women have slashed their wrists because their relationship ended.

The third strategy of the mind is to take a "stand against" something; I'm sure we're all familiar with this one. The mind sees something it doesn't like in the moment, and forms its opinion. Once we have a strong opinion, we tend to defend it. Beliefs become hardened, voices become loud and hearts close over. When we're in this mode we become mini-tyrants convinced of our own righteousness, and it is impossible for us to experience the moment in its depth and possibility. We know we're right, we know what we want and what we believe. This movement of the mind comes from overly identifying with our beliefs. If our beliefs are threatened, we feel threatened. Again the young child is activated in some way. The strong belief becomes a defensive shield that manifests as a controlling personality with a strong opinion and powerful voice. In reality, though, the fearful child is hiding behind the shield and is afraid to let go of it. Who are you without your beliefs?

Even religious or so-called spiritual people can have an evangelical attitude that effectively wants to tyrannize you with their fervent and righteous beliefs. We can't seem to let people be who they are without trying to change them in some way to suit our vision of how the world should be, just so the child in us can feel safe. This kind of thinking is very important on your CV if you are applying to be the next Mussolini or Hitler!

The mind will fight with the present moment in any way it can. If it can't find something 'out there' to fight with it will turn on itself and fight with its own thoughts. It's a bit like our dog Delilah, who bites her own tail. Or, a bit like me, when I used to be appalled at my own thoughts. A few paragraphs ago, my mind had dived into that woman's cleavage. Later, it would decide that it was appalled at its own thinking, and the internal narrative ran something like this:

> Inner Critic: "You shouldn't think thoughts like that. She's probably 15 years younger than you."
>
> Justification Thought: "Listen, she's very sexy, and she knows it. That blouse reveals a lot, and she's looking right into my eyes. It's OK.
>
> Inner Critic: "Hey, you're some piece of work. I mean, you're married! You shouldn't be staring at her cleavage and wondering what she would be like naked. You're a bad person."

You see how crazy-making it is when your mind is fighting with itself. If you try NOT to think about something, you end up thinking about it even more! It takes more mental energy to try to fight a thought than it does to ignore it.

And now, to make matters worse, there's a more insidious force at work underneath it all. It's the BIG LIE at the heart of the mind's machinations, and it's this – "THERE'S SOMETHING MISSING" or "THERE'S SOMETHING WRONG HERE."

It has spawned all of these smaller lies:

> "I need something to complete me."
>
> "There's something wrong with me."
>
> "I need to be more than I am."

"This moment, as it is, is not enough."

It is impossible to be at peace until you challenge this core lie. It can be directed inwards, "There's something wrong with me," – or outwards, "There's something wrong with life, with you, with them, with my job, with my marriage." It can't be happy with what's active in the moment (in the NOW), so it moves you away from NOW – and into the past or the future. It will activate a past wound, a grudge, a fear, a belief – and it will bring that into the present moment. Or it may simply move into the future and play out its fears there, causing you anxiety or worry in the present moment. This lie is one that is woven into the fabric of the life that the ego-mind has created for us, because without it the ego-mind would have no identity in and of itself. It would die. Many religions have used this lie as their foundation, and many of us have been tainted with the belief that there's something wrong in our very nature. This kind of thinking is insane, and it has caused a huge split in our psyche.

From an energetic point of view, here's what happens when the mind takes us into the future. It's quite subtle sometimes, so perhaps it's easier if, first of all, you focus on the Truth of this statement: "I AM HERE NOW." Breathe that statement into your lungs with each in-breath. Feel the resonance and truth of the statement. Feel your connection to the chair you're sitting on, or the ground beneath you, as you continue breathing. Now, pick a particularly anxious thought you might have about the future, and spend a little time with the thought (e.g. "What if…?").

Can you notice how the anxiety that the thought is creating is already causing you to lose your center? Your energy (power) begins to move out of your body towards the anxious future event. Your ego-mind is using your energy (power) to invest in a future negative. This movement of energy out of the body is particularly noticeable in the case of panic attacks – where the breath shortens, the body contracts or collapses in at the solar plexus area and the mind gets overloaded.

Any fear-based movement of mind causes your energy to move – from, towards or against. It takes time to develop the strange mixture of awareness, sensitivity and centeredness that allows you to notice how you are in the moment and what's happening in your mind. But it can be done. Be careful what you carry around in your head. If you look closely you'll see that you carry a lot of 'past' around with you. We haul tons of baggage around with us, subtly hidden in the layers of our existence, and sometimes not so hidden! Either way it's very tiring. When you don't hold onto time you travel lighter. You become more childlike and spontaneous, awake to each moment as it arises. Life begins to be a joyful experience for you, with the curiosity and wonder of a child learning from the wisdom and guidance of a great teacher. That teacher? It's NOW. It's every moment. It's life itself. The teacher is still waiting for you, with infinite patience. Are you ready to listen?

Exercise

As you breathe in "I AM HERE NOW" feel the truth of that statement. Breathe it into your lungs, into your belly and all the way down into your feet. Feel your connection to the ground beneath you.

Now, go back to that anxious thought, which is causing the feeling of anxiety somewhere in your body. Imagine the thought is a balloon with a string attached, and you're down here, while the balloon (thought) is 'up there' somewhere. The string is attached into your body somewhere. It may be curled up in your belly, wrapped tightly into a knot. It may be like a constant pulling upwards on your chest. It may be wrapped around your muscles somewhere. Register where in your body you're feeling the impact of that anxious thought. Remember that the string is attached into that feeling in your body. Now imagine that, as the balloon drifts higher and higher, the piece of string is lengthening, and the feeling begins to shift and unravel. The thought is approaching the clouds now. It's taking the string with it as it gradually unravels out of your body. You're here on the earth – and the balloon is way up there somewhere, but now you can't see it. It starts to disappear into the clouds. Take a deep breath and feel the breath entering your lungs. As you breathe in again, tell yourself, "I am ready to let go of this." Lastly, take one big breath in, and, as you now breathe out gently, you let go of the balloon and the string, and they disappear beyond the clouds as the feeling in your body dissolves too.

Chapter 10

I Am Evolving

I am ahead, I am advanced
I am the first mammal to make plans, yeah
I crawled the earth, but now I'm higher
It's evolution, baby
– Do the Evolution, Pearl Jam

You may think that you need to know your purpose. You may believe that you need something big to aim for. Well, I have news for you. Your purpose is not what you think you want, or what you feel you need. Your purpose is not what the world thinks you should want, or what your mind is programmed to want. Everyone thinks they want a better job, the perfect partner, more money, fame, but none of these things will make you happy on their own. There's nothing wrong with these things (money, success, the perfect partner), but these are not your purpose. Most likely they will happen AS A RESULT OF YOU FOLLOWING YOUR PURPOSE.

So what is your Purpose? I believe it's simply this – to EVOLVE. That's it! Your ego may be disappointed – but there it is. Your Purpose is to Evolve. That's what's happening all the time. The whole universe is evolving. Every species is evolving. If you're not, then you're basically saying NO to the incredible intelligence which runs through everything. It's a bit like this: your mind is saying, "OK, I recognize that the planets revolve around the sun, that we're hurtling through space at 86,000 miles per hour, and that tiny acorns grow into giant oak trees, and so on. Yes, yes, there seems to be a blueprint for everything – but that blueprint doesn't include me or my life. I know better. I'm taking over from here!"

We need to learn to cooperate with the deeper intelligence available to us that runs life itself and that some people call God. That intelligence (or God) is within us all. It's embedded in our DNA in the deep desire to evolve and grow. It asks you to wake up and grow beyond your limited beliefs and perceptions about yourself, and about the world as it is today. It asks you to allow 'all of who you are' to show up for life. It asks you to know your fears. It asks you to recognize your thought patterns and anything that robs you of joy. It asks you to let go, with love, of anything that keeps you restricted and limited and stuck. It asks you to step outside your comfort zones. It asks you to love deeply, and to embrace each moment. It asks you to EVOLVE.

But most of us don't want to evolve. Anthony De Mello called it "waking up," and he puts it like this:

Waking up is unpleasant, you know. You are nice and comfortable in bed. It's irritating to be woken up. That's the reason the wise guru will not attempt to wake people up. I hope I'm going to be wise here and make no attempt whatsoever to wake you up if you are asleep. It is really none of my business, even though I say to you at times, "Wake up!"

Yes, waking up will bring you challenges – but at least you're alive now! It will also bring you fulfilment and laughter. It may even bring you to ecstasy. It will certainly bring you to tears – tears of joy as you experience the incredible vibrancy and beauty of a simple flower, as well as tears of grief when you realize how often you abandon your true self. This is your purpose, to evolve. It means that you've got to be able to look at where you don't take full responsibility for your choices and for your thinking. It's easier to not take the responsibility to make conscious choices. It's easier to take the ride offered by the ego, fueled by the media and marketing empires. We can easily let them do our thinking for us. It's fascinating when you realize that it's not just religions that want you to think a certain way. Big business is heavily invested in making us believe we need things, or that certain things are somehow 'good' for us. Once we believe the hype, then they provide us with those 'things we need' which include anything from cigarettes to pensions, from the latest smartphone to a quick-fix tablet. We, the gullible consumers, fall for it every time! Here's a few things that we believed, or still believe.

"You're not cool if you don't smoke."

Yes, most of us fell for that one at some stage.

"You're suffering from blah-blah-blah syndrome. Just take this tablet for the rest of your life, and you'll be OK."

Yes, we all fall for this one still. It's easier to take Xanax, Anadin (Anacin), Prozac or Diazepam. We don't want to look at what's causing the problem. We don't want to look at ourselves or our habits. Maybe you're overweight. Oh well, just get yourself hypnotized or get a gastric band or some liposuction. Whatever you do, don't monitor what you eat and how little you exercise. Who, exactly, are we fooling? Maybe you're stressed because you're incredibly busy. No problem. Take these tablets so that you can CONTINUE to live the same busy life that's causing the stress in the first place!

All of this is built on the extremely appealing notion that you don't need to think for yourself or take responsibility for your life. Don't, whatever you do, take responsibility for the fact that you eat too much processed food. Don't, whatever you do, take responsibility for what you put into your body. Don't, whatever you do, take responsibility for not exercising and getting your heart rate up at least twice a week for 30 minutes. Don't, whatever you do, take responsibility for what you think and how that affects your life. After all, nothing is your fault. It's all someone else's fault, isn't it? In other words, have another cookie or another drink, numb out and blame something else or someone else. That's what we do. If you're overweight, stressed, anxious, too busy, in chaos (or all of the above!), you will want to run away and hide. You may run away and drown in alcohol, or food, or another relationship, or simply create some drama for temporary relief. In fact, you'll do anything at all to escape from the pain that you won't face up to. Running away becomes a pattern, and then you feel bad about yourself after finishing that bottle of wine. So your Inner Critic starts up again, and you start blaming yourself again – and the endless cycle continues.

In my own life I've seen these patterns. Yes, like you, I've been a slow learner too. Sometimes I had to reach my absolute limit before I learned the hard lesson. I remember one point in my life where my relationship was failing, my business was failing, and I felt I was failing as a father to my two daughters, who were still living with me. I was extremely stressed and unwell. I had been crying a lot over the previous few weeks, and I couldn't seem to stop it. It came in waves. Tears of "Poor me." Tears of "How could this happen?" Tears of "How do I get out of this?" Tears of deep loneliness and feelings of powerlessness. My girlfriend at the time convinced me that I needed to see a doctor. So along I went. I sat in the doctor's consulting room and talked for a few minutes about my life as it was at the time. Then my girlfriend spoke for about 20 minutes. She had a very strong and forceful personality, and was very clever with words. She could be very convincing. By the time she was finished the doctor had decided that I was suffering from depression. That was the first shock. Me? Depressed? The second shock was that she prescribed antidepressant tablets for me. Me? Antidepressants? My girlfriend was adamant that I had to take them, and that they would solve all my problems. All of a sudden I felt very vulnerable. Yet again I had somehow engineered a situation where I could easily believe something about myself just because someone else told me that's how it was. This was a pattern for me in most of my adult life. It was time to challenge it.

Half an hour later I was staring vacantly at the packet of antidepressants in my hand. The chemist had said that it was just a low dose, 20mg, she said. I remember looking at them and thinking, "How did it get to this? I'm not depressed." Yes, I had made some bad choices. Yes, I was doing things that didn't fill me with joy. Yes, I felt very controlled. Yes, this relationship sucks, but I can change that. My business sucks as well. I can change that too. I have a choice.

That's when it dawned on me. I had ALLOWED all of this to happen. I had allowed myself to be steamrolled into making decisions that didn't feel right to me. I had allowed myself to doubt my own intuition. I had handed my power over to others, and in the process I had lost myself. Why didn't I make decisions that reflected what I wanted? Had I disowned my own needs? Was I that unimportant to myself? Who was I if others were able to manipulate me into saying and doing things that went against every fiber of my being?

Who was Eoin? And where exactly was Eoin? Had he disappeared somewhere? Would he ever come back?

It was one of those turning points that many of us have experienced in our lives. I looked again at the antidepressants, and my powerlessness shifted up a gear. I suddenly felt very angry. It felt hot. My anger wanted me to stand up for my needs. It wanted me to reclaim my boundaries. This anger felt like it had wanted to scream NO a thousand times, but I had suppressed it. This anger had wanted me to walk away many times before, but I had ignored it. The anger felt a little frightening, although it was strangely comforting to know it was there. It was a whole lot better than collapsing into tears!

I looked down at the two little pills in the palm of my hand, and a scream welled up inside me. NO! I took the pills and flushed them down the loo. Then I walked over to the mirror and looked into my own eyes. I saw the angry me and the fearful me. I saw that the angry part of me had finally risen up and said, "I'm here to take care of that fearful part of you for a while." As I stared at my reflection I made a promise, one that I intend to keep for the rest of my life. I said to myself: "I WILL NEVER ABANDON MYSELF AGAIN. I WILL NEVER BETRAY MY OWN INTUITION, MY OWN INTEGRITY, MY OWN POWER. NEVER AGAIN!"

It felt good. It felt true. While it took me a while to make all the changes I needed to, I did it all. I kept reminding myself of the promise I had made to myself. It had taken me a long time to realize that I had been damaging myself by the choices I had made. My mind had seduced me into believing that someone else needed to change and that things 'out there' needed to change. The truth was that no one needed to change except me. It was never anyone else's fault. In fact, if I made it someone else's fault, then I was 'handing them the power.' The good news was that once I reached that AHA moment, I began to take responsibility – 'the ability to respond' – rather than feed the continuous cycle of reactive behavior. I had been reacting to reality as it was at the time, without recognizing that I had partly created it!

So I decided to let go of reactive behavior, and to move into creative behavior. It's a totally different paradigm when you finally stop focusing on what's not working and what you don't like. You stop feeding all that stuff with your own energy. You begin to recognize that your own needs are valid and that your desires are a very powerful catalyst for change. I also recognized that I had been afraid of facing up to the 'problems.' When I began to see what was really happening, I saw how I had allowed others to have 'authority' over me. The anger stopped all of that. When I finally threw those pills away and made my vows, I had activated the impulse to evolve. I was no longer stuck in a rut – a rut I had partly worn out for myself. Once I activated the impulse to grow, I felt my energy and power returning to me. It was as if I had handed all that energy and power over to others. We all do, you know. We hand our power to our fears. We hand our power to big business, to our partners, to anyone who will take it, because sometimes we don't want it. We don't want our power because that means we have to take responsibility for how we use it. We're afraid of how powerful we can be if we cooperate with our impulse to evolve and expand, rather than limit and constrict.

It's a wonderful thing, to cooperate with GOD, if you like, or with the EVOLUTIONARY PROCESS, or DIVINE INTELLI-GENCE. When you cooperate with it, you open up a whole new way of being. When you resist it, you cause yourself suffering because you're resisting the very force that both is you and wants the best for you. It knows the way.

The disciple went to visit the Master. He had a question.

"How does one seek union with God?"

"The harder you seek, the more distance you create between Him and you."

"So what does one do about the distance?"

"Understand that it isn't there."

"Does that mean that God and I are one?"

"Not one. Not two."

"How is that possible?"

"The sun and its light, the ocean and the wave, the singer and his song –

not one. Not two."

– Anthony De Mello

Exercise

1. Name one way you have given your power away.

_____

_____

_____

2. What thought or belief stops you from reclaiming your power?

_____

_____

_____

3. Are you ready to let go of that thought?

4. Use the exercise in the previous chapter (with the balloon) to let go of the limiting thought/belief.

5. Now you're ready to BE more powerful in your life. Use the Intention setting technique in Chapter 7, Just For Today, to anchor the feeling of being powerful. "Just for today, I am powerful. I love feeling my power. I love making decisions that are powerful for me."

Chapter 11

Fear Is Your Friend

"I have accepted fear as a part of life – specifically the fear of change … I have gone ahead despite the pounding in the heart that says: turn back."
Erica Jong

My mind has gone blank, my anxiety levels are at an all-time high – but I'm told that my legs moved and my body walked up to the front of the room, and my mouth opened! I don't remember much about it, but apparently there was a disembodied voice coming out of my mouth, squeaking in a high-pitched voice! That, my friends, was my first experience of public speaking – a Stage 1 'Ice Breaker' talk in Toastmasters, and it lasted an eternity – OK, OK – it lasted four minutes! But it felt like eternity! All I had to do was to simply tell the audience about me, in any way I wanted to. Can't be that difficult, can it?!!

But as the day approaches, the fear mounts. I haven't done it before. The closer the day gets, the more insecure and anxious I feel. The voices start whispering in my mind: "Why did you agree to this?" "You don't have to put yourself through this." I tried to ignore the voices, but they got louder. "You're no good at public speaking." "No one is interested in what you have to say!" And of course, "You'll make a fool of yourself." That went on for a few days until a more powerful voice emerged from deep down. This one was very angry. I remember it shouting back at the nagging fearful voices. "Shut up, I'm not listening anymore. I am going to do this thing, no matter what. So get lost!" My anxiety subsided for a while, and, a few days later, I made my way to the hotel. I bustled through the front doors and headed for the first floor via the stairs. I remember it well.

I walk up 25 steps. Yes, I do remember how many, because I counted each one as I tried my best to relax, but my breath grew tighter and more restricted. Anyone looking at me would think I was unfit, but I wasn't. I was scared. I look down the corridor and see the open door with a small desk just inside it. A pasty-looking woman with "Jessica" on her nametag, who looks like she's just blown in on a broomstick, asks me for some money. She scans me from top to bottom, and I'm convinced she can see how scared I am. I do my best to smile back but I keep thinking that she must smell the fear that's oozing from every pore in my body. Then she calls out, "Public Speaking virgin, eh, Eoin?" and I blush and stammer. "Fff-funny!" She knows! She smiles, takes my money and starts chatting to me as if I am normal. I'm not, but I pretend I am. Phew! The fear subsides a notch.

I decide to take a risk and tell Jessica how I feel. "If I was a nuclear reactor I'd be close to meltdown at this stage," I quip. "Everyone has some fear about their first time, don't they?" she says, with a tinkling laugh. "I suppose so," I said, but my laugh was more like a nervous release. Then a rather large man with an equally large personality comes over and is suddenly pumping my hand – "Hi Eoin, my name is Mike, and we're really looking forward to you tonight."

How does everyone know my name? Suddenly I feel very exposed and extremely ill-equipped to deal with all this attention. It's as if they're welcoming me to my own hanging! You know how it is. You've signed up to something that you've been putting off for a long time. There's a part of you that hopes the date will magically disappear somehow, or even better, that your fear will magically disappear. The event doesn't disappear. The fear is still there. All of a sudden the week arrives, the day comes, the hour approaches – and it's happening, actually happening, only it's like slow motion. Unreal. Your greatest fear is about to be unleashed and there's nothing you can do about it. Why? Because some time ago, in a fit of bravery, you decided to confront it.

So there I am, finally sitting down, with 40 people crammed into the hotel room. They all seem really relaxed as they listen to the introductions given by a rather stern woman named Kathy. All I can see is the clock on the wall as it inches inexorably towards SPEECH TIME, my time, action time. Kathy's voice fades out and I become aware that my body is feeling strangely heavy, my legs like dead weights, stuck to the ground. I look longingly at the exit door and know that I can leave, now, this instant! But something keeps me stuck to the chair. I stay. I've committed to this and I'm going through with it.

And then I hear it. My name announced from the front of the room, as all heads crane to catch a glimpse of THE PUBLIC-SPEAKING VIRGIN. Except the virgin hasn't moved! I'm still glued to the chair. My legs won't obey the command coming from my brain. The announcer scans the audience and repeats his invitation. "And now, please welcome Eoin Scolard, here to give his first ever talk, his ICEBREAKER tonight – Eoin Scolard." They all applaud. The man next to me prods me in the arm – and suddenly I'm up and off, like a greyhound after a rabbit, striding up the aisle at speed – and feeling as if I'm in a dream. Maybe I am. A nightmare perhaps. I can't feel my body anymore. Maybe I'll wake up soon.

I have to talk for four minutes. Foooouuurrr mmmmiinnuutteesss...... and then they switch on the red warning light if you talk for too long. That's the deal, part of the Toastmasters system. They start you off easy – four minutes to talk about yourself. No targets to hit, no need for presence, pause, pitch, patter, persuasiveness, power, passion, and that's just the P's! Just get up and talk, for God's sake, for four LONG minutes. So I do. I talk. I'm speaking. To be more accurate, I can hear a disembodied voice that sounds remarkably like me making some high-pitched sounds. More treble than bass. More squeaking than speaking. I'm making no eye contact as I gaze at the space above their heads, while my armpits stretch the capacity of the human body to produce water and salt! I'm still telling my story. Two minutes, three.

And then four! The nightmare is over. I suddenly wake up, standing in front of forty people. They clap. "Four minutes, ten seconds, not bad for your first time," pipes a smart ass in the front row. I'm red as a beetroot but I don't care. I start walking back to my seat, feeling exhilarated. Alive. My eyes are bulging as the sweat rolls down my forehead and collects in my eyebrows. But I really don't care. I've done it!

As I sit back down I get a few claps on the back while my body erupts with energy, that post-anxiety rush of adrenaline and excitement we're all familiar with when we try something outside our comfort zone. I did it! I did it! I settled into my seat and surreptitiously wiped my armpits with tissue as the next speaker was being introduced. My body began to cool down and my eyes retreated back into their sockets. It seemed to me that I had awoken a sleeping giant, a huge reservoir of energy that had been lying undiscovered, deep inside me, buried under layers of fear. Fear of making a fool of myself. Fear that no one would listen. Fear that I had nothing valuable to say. There were layers on layers of fear, all wrapped up in a lack of self-esteem sandwich that had been thoroughly toasted by lots of my formative experiences and subsequent limiting beliefs. I had made and eaten that sandwich many times. I remade it and kept eating it for most of my life. I never thought of making a new sandwich or eating a different one. Not until that day.

Looking back at it now I realize that I had learned a great lesson that day – that fear wasn't the problem. The fear was simply there, frozen in place like a giant ice cube inside me. What I needed to do was melt it and release the river that wanted to flow. It was, and always was, my choice whether to do anything about it or not, although for years my 'choice' was to do nothing. We've all done that. Hell, we're still doing it! We do nothing.

We're frozen, full of fear, like giant ice cubes! After a while we don't even realize it – because the fear itself is in control. And that's the problem. The fear takes over, freezes our lives and makes us dead to what we're capable of. It belittles us, and backs us into corners and dead ends, where there's no light and no space at all. It deadens our hearts, cramps our minds, stifles our emotions and tightens our bodies.

I've worked with many 'successful' people who have admitted to me that they were full of fear, despite the outward show of confidence. Sure, they had the big car and the big personality, the 'perfect' family, plenty of money. But inside there was no success at all. The outward stuff simply did a good job of hiding the fear. They were anxious about tomorrow, worried about their kids, insecure in their sexuality, scared about the possibility of illness or redundancy, old age or loss of financial security. And of course the more fearful they became, the more tightly they held onto what they had. Result? More stress and a greater need to control things.

I began to see that it's possible to fear anything, no matter how successful, how confident or self-assured we APPEAR to be. We have the amazing capacity to be afraid of anything. We can be afraid of starting a relationship, or ending a relationship! We can be afraid of being in a relationship, or being on our own! We can worry about having children, or having no children!

Anyhow, back to the story. Another lesson arrived at the coffee break. People came up to congratulate me on my first talk. They handed me their 'evaluation slips' too. These were small, preprinted postcards which Toastmasters uses to help you receive feedback and learn from it. Toastmasters recommends that people tell you something they liked about your talk, then make a suggestion for improvement, then tell you one other thing they liked. I noticed that a few people had commented on the fact that I didn't move from the spot. Others noticed that I rocked backwards and forwards, left and right and back again –

constantly! The funny thing was that I wasn't aware of that at all. In fact, I had almost no body awareness during my talk. I was feeling a bit despondent about this realization when a man came up and shook my hand, saying, "Well done, Eoin, that was great for your first time." "Really? I've been told that I was rooted to the spot, like a rabbit caught in the headlights." "Oh yes," he said, laughing, "you sure looked scared! A few of us were joking that we almost got seasick just watching you stand there, swaying left and right."

I laughed nervously, feeling very self-conscious and quite small.

I said, "That's terrible."

But then he said something that impacted me hugely.

"No, no, it's great. Really great."

"How so?" I asked.

"Well," he said. "You obviously had a lot of fear. I could hear it in your voice, which was high-pitched, nervous and out of control. All of that is normal. That was a whole lot of energy, which I guess you're not used to. Did you feel it when you sat down afterwards?"

I laughed and pointed to the pools under my armpits.

"Well," he said, "here's the secret. You can learn to use all that locked-away energy."

"What do you mean?" I asked eagerly.

He said: "You can put all that energy into your body movement, or you can use it to really emphasize your gestures or even direct it into deepening your voice. In fact, you can become a master of all that energy and use it in any way you want to during the talk. That's the real trick." He said, "Fear is your friend. You are in charge. Not the nervousness or the anxiety. You can feel all that energy and you can use it. It's the secret to becoming a really strong speaker."

Over the following weeks I pondered his words. So I had a lot of energy locked away. That much appeared to be true. And I sweated and swayed. That was true too. The fear did take me over so that I was disconnected from my body. That was also true. I began to understand that when I was aware of the fear AND NOT AFRAID OF IT, I could use it, rather than it using me. Those few words "Fear is your friend" opened me up to a new perception. Fear was showing me the edges of my comfort zone. That's all. If I wanted to grow as a person I would always meet my edges. I would know I was at my edge when fear kicked in. It wasn't the enemy at all. This felt good.

I was really looking forward to my next talk, which came after a month. This time I didn't repress or pretend that there wasn't anxiety or fear. I was able to tell myself that these were simply there, but that I was going to use all that emotional energy. By acknowledging and allowing myself to feel rather than repress, I opened up an untapped source of energy. I put all the fear and anxiety into my talk in different ways. I used my hands more. I moved around the stage. I varied my voice from boom to whisper. I emphasized my posture. As the talks progressed over an eighteen-month period, I became a master of all the unconscious energy that was hidden away under my fear. I was in charge; I was using all that pent-up energy to good effect. Wow!

I realized that I had spent many years not speaking up, repressing my own voice on many occasions. Now I knew why. It was like somebody else was in charge of a part of me. I remembered back to being a small boy who was shouted down or told to be quiet or not to contradict. I remembered the feeling of really wanting to be heard but being afraid in case I got into trouble. I remembered seeing things and not being allowed to discuss them. I remembered not understanding other things and not feeling safe enough to talk about them. Somehow I learned that my voice wasn't important and that staying quiet was preferable. This became my default position. As an adult I simply continued to embody that behavior. Now I finally realized that it wasn't the real me. There was an energized authoritative communicator hiding in there underneath it all! The more I thought about it the more sense it made. That little boy inside me was ready to shout, from the rooftops if necessary!

I began to apply this lesson to any time I was working through emotional or psychological fear. I'm not talking here about the intelligent physical fear that we need in order to survive some situations. When confronted directly with a threat to its survival, the body responds accordingly with a fight or flight response. That's a direct and instinctual response to an external situation, so let's not confuse that response with any fear-based emotion. An emotion is not a direct instinctual response. It's the body's response to a thought.

Having learned this, I began to focus on acceptance of whatever I was feeling inside. The more I did this, the more authentic I felt and the better I felt about myself. I was beginning to take charge of my life. I recognized that I had a large number of fears but I also saw that I wasn't alone. Everyone experienced fear! I recognized that there was a huge storehouse of energy waiting to be reclaimed if I faced my fears. But most of us won't admit to what's really going on inside. We fear loss, abandonment, responsibility, rejection, intimacy, change, disapproval, truth, looking stupid, lack, conflict, self-expression, being emotionally honest, and another few thousand fears! We avoid these fears by compensating or pretending. After a while we don't even recognize what we're doing or why we're doing it. We get stuck on autopilot, and we don't even know where we're going! We end up being ashamed of our fear-based thoughts, and fearing our feelings too!

And so we build up a false image of ourselves, one that is usually based on either the fight or flight response. The real you has died somewhere along the way. You may compensate by developing a big personality that says, "I don't do fear." You may retreat into yourself and simply deny your feelings. You may stay in the comfort zone of the familiar. But it's not you. It's a fake you, a pretend you that takes a lot of energy to maintain. It will eventually drain you.

So my message to you is simple but challenging. It's time for YOU to be YOU. Stop pretending, stop complaining, stop procrastinating, stop doing **anything** that is based on fear. Yes, I know it's a real challenge – so you need to make it easy on yourself. Make sure that you'll be setting yourself up for success. Remember that the fear wants you to fail and then say, "I told you so."

Fill in the following few lines as spontaneously as you can.

Exercise

I'M AFRAID OF BEING

_____

_____

_____

I'M AFRAID TO (something you want to do)

_____

_____

_____

My advice is to start with something small you have been avoiding like making that phone call that isn't too scary. Gradually work up to the bigger stuff that may be a bit scarier. Make a commitment to do something psychologically/

emotionally frightening once a week, until your courage muscle gets noticeably stronger and your self-esteem grows. Notice what happens each time you face the fear, and how you feel afterwards. Focus on that good feeling. Anchor the new feeling in some way, so that it becomes integrated. Write about it. Get out your markers and draw pictures of the 'bigger you.' Remember that the fear has an agenda to keep you small, insignificant, constricted and stuck. And remember too that it's effectively someone else's agenda, buried in your past. It's just that you haven't learned what to do with fear yet. How could it be your own agenda? Nobody wants to be small and disempowered, not at their core. Sure, you may feel that from time to time, but it's not you. It can't be. You are pure potential, in seed form. Every time you stand up to the fear you nurture that seed and begin to break out of the shell. Every time you break through a fear you feel better about yourself, simply because the real you is emerging. It's a very juicy feeling!

The process looks something like this. First comes AWARENESS. You've got to develop the muscle of awareness, always noticing what's happening inside you, in your body, mind, emotions and spirit. Anytime you notice constriction or restriction, tightness, closure, defense or withdrawal, that's fear! Then comes ACCEPTANCE AND MAKING FRIENDS WITH YOUR FEAR. Accept the fear, whatever it is… perhaps making that difficult phone call… or saying three little words… or joining a dating site… and so on. Don't judge your fear. Don't label yourself as wrong in any way. Say "Hello" to that part of you that feels afraid. Make friends with your fear. I often speak to myself this way: "Hello, FEAR, I see you there, lurking in the shadows. Come on out so we can have a chat." Reassure that part and tell it you're ready to feel all the fear and anxiety. Next comes CHOICE AND COMMITMENT. Sometimes we find it difficult to make a decision. We torture ourselves endlessly about it, we procrastinate about it, we sit on the fence. We can end up like the proverbial donkey between two bales of hay, and we starve to death! We think, "I might make the WRONG decision," as if that's a good enough reason to not take action! Just for today, I want you to shift your thinking so that making a wrong decision is impossible. Develop the kind of thinking that tells you, "No matter what decision I make, it's the right one. Making a wrong decision is impossible. Whatever happens as a result of my decision is perfect for me and I will learn from it, whatever happens." Whatever decision you make, commit to it completely.

So, let's apply these tips to real life. You've been thinking of moving on in a situation, but fear has kept you stuck, powerless and miserable! You just can't make a decision. You keep thinking, "What if?" and you go around in circles. First you shift your thinking to, "I can't make a wrong decision." Having gathered up all the data and weighed up all the pros and cons and tuned into your gut instinct, you then make your decision. Whatever you decide, DO NOT go back to thinking about the other possibility. Invest ALL your energy in the decision you've made, whatever that is.

Next comes the exciting part. ACTIVATE AND TRANSFORM. You're aware of the fear – there it is. You've accepted it and made friends with it and chosen what to do. Now you activate and transform the fear when you take the action… by making the phone call… by speaking your truth… by arranging for an interview… whatever it is that needs to happen. Notice how you feel when you commit to something and follow through despite the fear. Most people will be part-exhilarated and part-scared. While we allow both, it's the exhilarated part we want to focus on! The more we focus on that, the bigger it gets, the more powerful and 'normal' it becomes for you. There's a real sense of excitement when you connect in with that part of you that really wants to grow your wings, that part of you that wants to break free!

You'll see how powerful it feels to finally say what you need to say, or do what you need to do. The extra bonus is that you feel great about yourself. You're starting to take charge. Yes, you will feel all kinds of emotional and physical reactions, before and after the action. That's normal. Just notice what's going on. That's your job now, just to notice. "Ah, here comes a little shakiness and tightness of breath." No problem. "Here comes my mind saying – You can't do it." No problem. Just notice those thoughts and feelings, and keep going.

I remember doing a firewalk when I was on a seven-day workshop in the Highlands of Scotland in 2005. Walking on fire is a strange pastime, I know, but hey, we're all uniquely peculiar! When you tell some people you've signed up to do a firewalk, they look at you as if you're slightly mad. I remember doubting my sanity too during one of the 'warm-up' exercises. We had to break an arrow in half by pushing the soft part of our throats against the tip of the arrow, until the arrow broke! I managed to get through all of the physical and psychological preparation.

What I remember most of all, besides the intense heat of the fire, the constant drumming and the slightly surreal surroundings, was the instruction that was firmly relayed to us.

"Set an intention for someone else. Do this for someone or something else. Whether you call it a prayer or intention, it doesn't matter. Do not walk until you have deeply connected with your prayer. Imagine the intention at the far side of the fire, and when you feel the pull, the draw of the intention, then you walk. You won't even see or feel the fire."

I remember this so vividly as the flames danced and the drumming took hold in the marrow of my soul. I remember the moment when all doubt vanished, when something deep inside me said, "Yes, this is your time now. Go for it." I remember walking across the fire towards my intention, without doubt, without fear. I remember feeling exhilarated when I reached the other side, realizing that I had the same courage I saw in others.

Here's some of the things I used to be afraid of:

Fear of… feeling some emotions, particularly sadness, grief and anger.

Fear of… showing or expressing my emotions.

Fear of… experiencing someone else's anger.

Fear of… Truth – speaking it and hearing it spoken to me.

Fear of… Failure.

Fear of… not having Enough.

Fear of… the Future.

Fear of… the opinions of others.

Fear of… being alone.

Fear of… speaking up.

Fear of… looking foolish.

Most of us have a large reservoir of energy buried underneath our fears. It's really exciting when you begin to mine this energy, and the first step is to be honest with yourself. This little exercise will help.

Complete the following sentences below, quickly and spontaneously. If you found yourself hesitating, perhaps your first fear is… Fear of being spontaneous! (I call this Stage 1 thinking, where we're so identified with our thought that we believe it to be true.)

I'm afraid to

_____

_____

_____

I'm afraid of

_____

_____

_____

I'm afraid to

_____

_____

_____

Notice that there's two parts of 'you' here. There's got to be. One part of you wants to break free and another part of you is holding you back. Your job is simply to see that there's two things going on. Don't worry about any future-based questions. Don't worry about, "How will it all work out?" or "What will happen if…?" These questions don't matter yet. "WHY?" is far more important.

Do you want to break through the fear? Why? In other words, what's on the other side? Will it give you more energy, more fulfilment? YES! Will you feel better about yourself? YES! Even the writing down of your fears lessens their hold over you straightaway. You get to see how they rob you of your truth and your power, and ultimately, your deep enjoyment of and connection to life. Remember that it's only a 'part' of you that's scared and fearful. The other part of you is powerfully waiting for you, on the other side.

Let's use me as an example. A few months after my marriage broke up, I made a decision, one of my better ones! I decided not to enter any intimate relationships for a full year, so that I could step back and learn what I needed to. When that year had passed I allowed myself to dream of meeting someone, but I had no real experience of relationships. All I had was a few teenage gropes, a 19-year marriage and an incredibly stupid crush which didn't last long. So, in reality I entered one relationship when I was 19, and I exited 22 years later!

Here I was, a year separated, 42 years of age, with zero experience of dating and all that goes with it. I didn't know what to expect and I didn't know what women expected. When I checked in with myself I saw that I was afraid to even allow myself the thought of another relationship. I felt scared by the thought of any physical contact – even my arm draped over a shoulder, or holding hands – but at the same time, I wanted it. This is what it's like for most of us when it comes to fear. There's a battle going on inside.

I identified the thought as: "I'm afraid to get close to a woman." Then I was able to break that down into the two parts – "The fearful part of me is afraid to get close to a woman," and "The excited part of me wants to get close to a woman."

I had arrived at that choice point where I could choose which part of me to energize – the fear or the excitement. I chose the excitement! I enrolled in salsa classes, turned up on my own and was chucked instantly into a woman's arms and shown the basics. Job done!

So, let's go back to your first statement (A), and write down exactly the same words as you did in your Stage 1 Thinking – in both instances below.

Statement A

The fearful part of me is afraid to

_____

_____

_____

And... The excited part of me wants to

_____

_____

_____

So now you've written down the same words, but you've changed the "I'm afraid to" to "The fearful part of me is afraid to." Once we've acknowledged that part of us, we've broken our identification with the fear. It's not "I" that's afraid at all – it's just "a fearful part." When we see that, it becomes very obvious that there's an excited part of us waiting there, hiding in the fear itself. The fear restricts us and keeps us closed. The excitement, based on what we want and desire, is there to do the opposite – to open us up. So, we fill in the very same words after, "The excited part of me wants to..."

Now look at what you've written. Both are true statements for you, so there's two parts of you wanting to be in charge of your life. Do you want a fearful life or an exciting life? It's your choice.

Now let's make a decision and stick to it, and let the heady mix of fear and excitement do their little dance inside you. Fill in the very same words you've already written again – this time after "I

AM READY TO" below – and notice what happens inside. Notice the mixture of the two parts, of fear and excitement, and pay more and more attention to the excitement.

I AM READY TO

_____

_____

_____

Congratulations! You've committed to doing something new, something that breaks the stranglehold of fear on a part of your psyche. Now do the same process for Statements B and C that you filled out.

Statement B

The fearful part of me is afraid of

_____

_____

_____

And... The excited part of me wants to

_____

_____

_____

DECISION: I AM READY TO

_____

_____

_____

Statement C

The fearful part of me is afraid to

_____

_____

_____

And... The excited part of me wants to

_____

_____

_____

DECISION: I AM READY TO

_____

_____

_____

Remember too that the only way to conquer fear is to go ahead and DO the very thing that you're afraid to do. That's why *Feel the Fear and Do It Anyway* was such a massive best-seller for Susan Jeffers. What you're actually doing is saying to the small you: "You're not in charge anymore" – and as you take the action, you meet with the bigger, more powerful part of you that's been there all along! Yes, you'll feel fearful at the time, but the fear is now turning into power and excitement as you take action! Enjoy the ride!

Here's a few more sentences to help you get in touch with some of your fears. Be curious about why you don't follow through.

I'd love to tell

_____

_____

_____

I'd love to try

_____

_____

_____

I'd love to start

_____

_____

_____

I'd love to stop

_____

_____

_____

One of the things that keeps me vibrant and excited about life is trying new things. So why not do it? Try something new each week. Take a risk. At the very least, it will make you feel alive! I often ask my clients to take a small risk before they come back to me for their next session. Here's what some of them have reported back with:

> I usually bitch about what my husband doesn't do. My risk was to notice what he does do, and to tell him that I appreciated him for those things. I even went so far as to give him a big hug. I know it's not earth shattering, but believe me, it's well outside my comfort zone! Four weeks later and he's helping out more than he ever did with the kids and the house. I can't believe the change in him!

As you've probably realized, this woman changed first, and THEN he changed. She took a risk. She changed. As she moved into appreciation and gratitude, he began to respond. That's what happens when you look at a situation and ask yourself, "What am I not giving?" rather than our usual, "What am I not getting?" In the Christian tradition, it's akin to, "Take the log out of your own eye before you take the speck out of your partner's eye."

Another client's feedback:

> I decided my risk this week was to not give the kids instructions or orders in the morning rush to school. They always

react badly, I get very stressed. Sometimes I lose my head! So I decided not to tell them what to do. I decided to ask them questions and to make requests instead. I was prepared to be late to school and to be refused my requests, but that didn't happen. We got to school on time, homework and tidying up was done without shouting or arguments, and they even practiced piano without me constantly nagging them. I relaxed, they relaxed, and the atmosphere in the house was a lot more relaxed! I've learnt that I can let go and not try to control everything – and life will still go on.

As well as modelling for her children that it was OK to be relaxed about life, this brave soul also gave her children a lovely message, "Mum trusts us to do our stuff."

This next feedback is from a woman in her thirties who was socially anxious but longed to meet someone for friendship and possibly a relationship:

My 'risk' for this week was to go to a work event this evening (formal – long dress – the lot!) – and not drink wine! When I got there I felt my fear and did it anyway. I joined in with a conversation with a fellow colleague that I didn't know – something that makes my palms sweat just thinking about it! We got talking and discovered we both enjoy the gym. We're members of the same club! We've met up a few times since and now we try to train with each other at least once a week. Who knows what the future holds!

One of mine:

This week I faced my fears and told my father that I loved him, something I always wanted to do but didn't. It opened up a whole new dimension in our relationship, and he shared things with me that he had never told anyone else.

Action Steps This Month

Look at the next four weeks. Make a decision every week to take the risk of freeing yourself from one of your fears. It can be anything you like – a phone call – starting a new class – trying something you've always put off – taking a small step towards something bigger. Each time you plan a risk and follow through, you're building resilience along with a new capacity to challenge anything that keeps you small. So, enjoy!

Chapter 12

A Letter To You

Dear Reader

You don't know me, but I control you. I'm so close to you that I'm invisible. That's my greatest trick. You see, most of you don't know I exist at all. I play you every day but you don't know it. I convince you of things that help me to control you more and more and you succumb so easily! That's how far I've progressed in my quest to control you and win the battle for your soul.

My name? I have many names. Some people call me The Dark One... The Lie... The Devil... The EGO... but the names don't really matter. In all honesty (and that's not one of my strong points) I prefer being unknown. I'm simply a lack of consciousness in the same way that darkness is just the absence of light. I operate anywhere in the Universe where conscious beings exist because, it being a Universe of opposites, there has to be unconsciousness too. I feed on your unconsciousness.

I live and thrive in the dark recesses of your mind, anywhere at all where you judge, criticize, or reject your thoughts, your emotions or your body, or anyone else's! I especially love it when you're right and they're wrong, or when you're good and they're bad, or when you fight with yourself. I love it when you argue and fight. I get really happy when you start wars based on your own inability to see the other in yourself. I love it when you make enemies and kill for your beliefs, especially your beliefs in your very own God! It's a hoot!

I usually start quite young, so that you don't even notice. That's how clever I am. I often begin with comparison and competition. That fosters jealousy, and I like that a lot. After a while I move on to resentment and bitterness, and I like them even more. I get you to strive for your parents' affections by doing only what they approve of. That gives me a foothold in you. You start to believe that you have to act or be a certain way to get love. After that? Well, to be honest, you're putty in my hands.

When you grow up and continue to believe you're not enough, I really get off on that! Why? Because your belief in all of these things gives me power. Thanks! I have so much power these days, all thanks to you – the human race. If you want me to thrive even more in your unconscious, keep on doing what you're doing and believing what you believe! I love the drama and misery on the pages of your newspapers, the wars and atrocities, the hungry egos, all in the name of… what? Power? Control? Don't be silly – I have all that, and it's all thanks to you.

Thanks again. Thanks for being afraid of change. Thanks for keeping secrets. Thanks for lying. Thanks for being afraid of truth and vulnerability. Thanks for identifying with your thoughts and beliefs. Thanks, most of all, for not taking responsibility for what you're creating in your little world. You're feeding me every day, and I am grateful. I am growing even more powerful – all because of you.

Always Yours
The Ego

Chapter 13

Dark, Light and Shadow

Hello darkness, my old friend,
I've come to talk with you again.
– The Sound of Silence, Simon and Garfunkel
(I prefer the slightly creepy version by Disturbed!)

Most of us were programmed from a very young age. Our early influences taught us that when we were good we were rewarded. When we were bad we were punished. So we learned to show the good side and to keep those bad bits of us hidden away in the Shadow. 'Bad,' by the way, is anything that you learned was not OK. Maybe you told the truth about something, and one of your parents told you off for opening your mouth. So you learned that speaking the truth was bad and you put that into the Shadow. Maybe you were so happy another day that you burst into the house singing at the top of your voice – and promptly got slapped by your mother. So you put spontaneity into the Shadow. This is what happens when a part of you is denied, and hidden away. It's useful to imagine your whole being as a seesaw, and that we balance the seesaw between those parts that we find acceptable and those we don't. The problem happens when we identify too much with one side and we ignore the other. We are 'so nice' (on one side) that we don't allow ourselves to feel the other side of that, perhaps our anger and resentment, until one day it explodes! We see that a lot in news coverage these days, where the neighbors are interviewed after a gruesome discovery about the young man in No. 19: "He was such a nice quiet boy, never did any harm to anyone. I just don't understand how he could have killed his parents like that."

While I'm not suggesting that we're all killers, I am suggesting that we all suppress and deny some aspects of ourselves. Many of us continue holding up our self-image at the expense of our deeper truth. We pretend to others that there's no darkness in us – and, eventually, all that pretense takes its toll. We need to acknowledge all aspects of ourselves, and to find ways to give expression to those aspects, in a healthy way.

I remember when my boss picked me up on something inconsequential in the finances of the company that I hadn't pointed out to him. I didn't show him how angry I felt. I kept it hidden away in the shadow. Although I felt very frustrated at the time I didn't know how to feel it and express it without losing my cool. So I went over and over the conversation in my head for the rest of the day. I was doing something which the psychologists call ruminating, a destructive mental habit which repeatedly relives an experience in your mind. You replay it and review it, reinterpreting it ad infinitum. "What should I have said? If I had said that, what would he have said? Why didn't I speak up? Why am I such a wimp?"

I didn't enjoy the rest of the day, and neither did my staff. I was short-tempered and cold with them all. Later on, as I inched through the Dublin traffic, I was still stuck in the past, replaying the whole event. I cursed a few drivers through my windscreen and I raged at the innocent cyclists: "You think you own the road. Did you not see that red light? It's red for a reason, you plonker!" By the time I got home, I was fuming, and of course, somebody had to have it!

What just happened? Psychologists call it displaced aggression, or postponed and redirected anger. Most of us recognize it as the kick-the-dog effect! By the time you get home, you're ready to blow. You park your car and stomp up the driveway. The front door opens and out pops your friendly little terrier who somehow manages to get under your feet and almost trips you up. You snap, your leg lashes out and you kick the dog! Two minutes later you realize what you've done, and you feel like a prize idiot.

It seems that we can easily get stuck in this mental habit of rumination, but it doesn't help. Replaying the annoying episode over and over just makes it worse. While you may think you're trying to understand it better, you may actually be keeping the frustration and anger alive. Hours later, even though you might not feel physically angry, the painful story is still there in your mind. You can't retaliate against your boss for obvious reasons. You can't take it out on the cyclists and car drivers unless you're OK with road rage! So, hours after the incident, anything even slightly annoying will trigger you. Ergo, the dog gets it!

What you need is some time to play out the anger and to let it breathe a little. One of my favorite ways to let off steam is to get into the car and turn the music up very loud. Then I scream the lyrics or make up my own expletive-laden lines. Alanis Morissette has some tracks that are great for anger – *Versions of Violence, Spineless, (The Only Way) Out Is Through*.

Some people find her lyrics almost too honest, but anything loud and angry will do. AC/DC and Metallica work well for some. The trick is to feel the emotion WITHOUT THE STORY. It's the ruminating and retelling of the story that fuels even more anger. Psychologists have theorized that if you continue to focus on anger-provoking situations you will form new angry associations, setting up a vicious circle of anger and further rumination. Because part of anger often involves self-justification, all you're doing is feeding the anger with more fuel, particularly when you keep on thinking of reasons why you were right, and he or she was wrong. As for the dog? Well, it probably knows that you just needed to blow your top, and as all dogs do, it will continue to love you.

If we continue to refuse the shadow, either personally or collectively, then we run away from the beauty and sacredness in us, as well as store and accumulate the darkness. The front pages of our newspapers reflect this shadow when we read about wars and atrocities, cover-ups and corruption. We invest our Shadow in all the horrible things that happen in the world, rather than integrating it in our own personalities. Projection is easier than assimilation!

So we need to 'make friends' with our own shadow and reintegrate all parts of ourselves. Our spiritual traditions need to reflect this as we move away from the traditional models of hierarchical religion which thrived on fear. We believed that we were defective somehow and that we needed redemption. We do need redemption but in a different way. Not through anyone else. Not by giving our power away to an institution.

Our redemption comes when we are willing to enter those spaces inside us that we have rejected. We need to learn how to love all the aspects of ourselves that have remained hidden for so long. In this way we reclaim our wholeness and begin to heal the split inside us. We learn to listen more deeply and to allow our truth to unfold as we find our way to our own authentic spirituality. A spirituality that accepts, loves and embraces ALL of who we are, including our Positive and Negative Shadow sides. This level of acceptance and unconditional self-love is very challenging to us. What happens is that life will bring you people who push your buttons and show you where your shadow is. In those situations the tendency is to view the other in a judgmental way. We need to be conscious enough to step back from any internal reaction to whatever their behavior sparks in us, and to look at our reaction. Somewhere in there is an aspect of our shadow. The more we can do this, the more we realize that life is set up in such a way that it's actually inviting us to get to know ourselves more deeply!

Even if our intention comes from love, what happens if the other person is not willing to receive that love? If we react to that then our ego is still involved. We may see it as an affront and we can take it personally. This type of love is not unconditional. It's the type of love that wants something from the situation. The love is conditional on getting something back from the other person, even if it's just an acknowledgment of how good a person we are. This is conditional love. It's the type of love that the vast majority of us have grown up with.

Arriving at the place where I could unconditionally love myself is not something that happened overnight. It has taken me years and years of journeying deep into the hidden part of my psyche, along with some ego-shattering experiences! Before you can love others, you've got to love the enemies inside yourself. Your ego will see many things inside you as an enemy. It may see weakness and vulnerability as an enemy. It may see your sexual fantasies as an enemy. It may see power as an enemy. You may not be able to love all these internal enemies, but you do have to acknowledge that they're there.

In the outside world, you may have enemies too and you may aspire to loving them too. That doesn't mean you have to like them, let alone spend a lot of time with them! There are people in my past that I choose not be around, people that I used to resent and judge harshly in my mind. Now that my ego is not in control so much, I can love them and include them in my prayer and meditation practice, although I don't want to be around them all the time. They may never know that I send them love. That's how it should be. Perhaps this is the ultimate goal, to love unconditionally. "Love your enemies. Forgive them, they know not what they do." It takes a long time to integrate that into the fabric of your everyday existence and it starts, of course, with yourself. It has to, because you cannot give what you don't have. When the air hostesses show the passengers on the airplane how to use the oxygen mask, they tell us to put the oxygen mask on ourselves first, and then look after others. We cannot give unconditional love unless we have it inside for ourselves. This is a lot to ask of us but it's what we're called to.

In my own journey I have found it easier to recognize all the times when I'm not coming from unconditional love than to recognize the times I am. I can tell you that the deeper you go into the areas where you don't hold that unconditional love for yourself, the more vibrant, alive and happier you become. What greater gift can you give yourself than discovering all the places in you that are still unforgiving, closed, wounded? You will be giving yourself the gift of freedom from the ego and the shadow. You will move into freedom from all of the negativity and fear that the world is so invested in. I don't believe there is a greater gift you can give yourself.

My journey has shown me that Life itself is seeking to bubble up and be expressed through us. You can substitute God, or Spirit, or Consciousness, for the word "Life" in that sentence. Experiencing that is one of the most beautiful things you can do for yourself. One of the gifts of being human is the gift we have of conscious choice. It's a bit like the Adam and Eve story. You choose. What fruit will you eat? What belief will you go with? Will you pick the usual belief that you need more 'stuff' to be happy? Will you pick the fear-based, consumer and drama world that you somehow know is not good for you? Or will you choose to be in the world, but not of it?

If we pick the good fruit we learn to cooperate with life itself. There is a tremendous ease in this type of living. It's not a living of the mind, efforting and trying to better ourselves. It's not taking hold of any religious belief or ideology and trying to superimpose that on our lives. At a deep spiritual level, we don't need to strive for anything. We need to surrender to life itself and cooperate with it. As Eckhart Tolle puts it:

> Life will give you whatever experience is most helpful for the evolution of your consciousness. How do you know this is the experience you need? Because this is the experience you are having at the moment.

This doesn't mean that we become any particular 'ideal' person.

We don't need to be quiet or holy or spiritual or whatever you think you SHOULD be. It doesn't mean that we have to sit on top of a mountain and meditate every day. It simply means that we are part of the wonderful dance of Life, and that we can have a deeper awareness of that in every moment, understanding that Life is inviting us to live a fully human connected life. That means that we don't push away or reject any aspect of life that comes to us.

There's a Zen story of a young monk who came to the Master to pay homage.

"I beg you, Master, to show me your compassion and lead me to freedom. Show me how to be free."

"Go and find who has bound you," said the Master.

The monk came back after a week.

"No one has bound me," said the monk.

"That being the case," said the Master, "why should you continue to seek for freedom?"

And, in that moment, the monk awakened to the truth, that no one had bound him. He was free, except for the imaginary chains he had placed on himself. Imaginary. That's the key word here. We're all like that young monk, thinking that something is constricting our freedom. We're also like the camels arriving at the oasis, in a different story:

A camel trader was walking across the desert, and pitched a tent for the night. The slaves drove pegs into the ground, and tied the camels to the pegs. Then they came in to say to the master:

"There are only nineteen pegs and we've got twenty camels. What will we do?"

The master said:

"These camels are stupid animals. Just go through the

motions of tying the camel up."

So they pretended to tie the camel up, and he stayed put all night. The next morning the slaves began to set off until they realized that all the camels were following, except this same one, who refused to budge, even though there was no rope on him. They went to the master for a solution.

The master said:

"That camel doesn't know that he is free. Go through the motions of untying him. Then he'll be fine."

So they did, pretending to untie him. Only then was he free to move!

You are always free unless you choose to believe that you're not. It's that simple. You are free. The problem is that you don't believe you are free. You allow an idea to get a hold of you and tie you up. All of a sudden you're like the camel. Maybe you think you have to HAVE something. That can tie you up. "I have to have that," says the ego. "Now go and get it," says the world. "When you get it you can regard yourself as successful." What happens? You go to get it, whatever it is, a relationship, a better job, a pay raise. You're not happy until you get it so your life is on hold for now. Eventually, one of two things will happen. You will either fail or you will succeed. If you fail, the ego gets very involved. "You're useless," it says. "Try again." Alternatively, if you succeed, the ego also gets involved. "You're a success," it says. Your ego identifies with that, and for a while, you feel happy. That new job or extra money gave you great joy, didn't it? But how long before the ego says, "Hey, I'm kinda bored with this. Now go get something else, or get a bigger, faster, newer model." It's a lose-lose situation.

Kipling's inspiring poem "If" captured this as far back as 1895:

If you can dream – and not make dreams your master;
If you can think – and not make thoughts your aim;

If you can meet with Triumph and Disaster
And treat those two impostors just the same.

Having to have something can tie you up, just like the camel. Then you're not free. You have to have it, whatever it is. There's an unconscious belief at work here and it goes like this, "I need to HAVE more so I can DO more so that then I can BE happy." It's called the DO-BE-HAVE paradigm, and most of us have it in the wrong order.

The belief that you need to have MORE of anything will always be in charge of HOW YOU ARE. This belief makes sure that you'll never be happy with what you have. You have to have more. You have to have success. You have to have a bigger better car, house, whatever. Don't get me wrong. I love having things too, but my happiness is not dependent on them. How do I know? Because I've lived through having very little. I've lived through negative equity, where I could have easily declared bankruptcy. In my life I've HAD a lot and I've also HAD very little. I'm not that interested in 'having' as the starting point for anything I do. Whether you're rich or poor doesn't matter. If you're poor you look at rich people and believe that you have to have what they have. Then you'll be somebody! If you're rich you can be subtly fearful of losing your wealth. Then you'll be nobody! Either way, your very BEING is held hostage to the need to HAVE.

Our core longing is not to HAVE, but to BE. Wanting something different to what's actually happening is the greatest obstacle to our happiness. It takes us away from the moment. It's the root of greed and envy, anxiety and stress. It happens when we identify so much with 'HAVING' that we lose touch with our sacredness and the sacredness of all life – which is the foundation of any true spirituality. This does not negate the desire to have things or for things to change, but it is desire WITHOUT attachment. This subtle difference is the key to understanding how life moves towards us in an organic way, rather than our egos getting involved, forcing or pushing. When we allow ourselves to be happy in the moment, the Universe comes to meet us and we begin the co-creative dance.

The second part of this DO-BE-HAVE paradigm is our belief that we somehow need to DO more so we can HAVE more. Then, finally, we can BE happy. Many people have spent entire lifetimes in jobs that don't fulfil them so that they can HAVE their pension. Then, after forty years of stress and unhappiness, they'll BE happy. Forty years! Madness!

Both instances are the wrong way around. Both lead to stress and anxiety, worry and attachment. You've got to put BEING first, not HAVING or DOING. When BEING comes first, there's no success or failure. There's no stress, no should, ought to, have to. There's simply BEING. You simply ARE. When this BEING permeates and integrates into every moment, then it turns up in all the aspects of your life, whether that's washing the dishes, making love, stuck in a traffic jam, meeting somebody whose personality you find difficult, coping with the death of a loved one, coping with your own illness, or anything at all that life offers you.

I'll use this book as an example. I have been writing this book for a few years now. I'm not DOING it so that I HAVE success and lots of money. They may happen, as by-products of my writing. It's also quite possible that this book will never be published, or that I will have to self-publish it, and that it only sells a few hundred copies. I have no idea what will happen. Even if I somehow knew it was only going to sell a few hundred copies I would still write it, because it is arising out of my BEING. Musicians and artists are usually the same. They simply have to create. They are BEING first. The DOING and HAVING are secondary by-products of BEING. When you're fully connected to BEING, happiness simply IS. Fulfilment simply IS.

I am fully surrendered to BEING with this creative process.

It's as if this book cannot NOT be written, like a child who, after nine months in the womb, just HAS to be born. What happens afterwards, I don't know. Will anyone read it? I sincerely hope so, but I'm not in control of that. I've done my part by writing it, and sure, I'll get the best possible advice about agents, publishers and all of that. But the writing was always the point of these four years. I am 'giving' what needs to be expressed through me at this time. When you give like this, you know that there is no lack. You're not waiting for something to happen. You're like the rose, freely giving its perfume to whoever passes by. However, if you give purely for personal gain, or in the expectation of getting something back, then your giving is all about getting. Be honest with yourself. Whatever you're doing, what are you getting out of it? Be ruthlessly honest, even though your ego won't like it.

Check your DOING for its foundation. DOING founded on 'getting' is based on some unconscious belief that WHEN I get such and such, THEN I'll be happy. "When I get that job, that house, that partner, promotion, that fame, that recognition, then I will be successful, happy, fulfilled." In other words, the unconscious belief is that you need these things in order to be happy. Your unconscious needs will run your life until you bring them into consciousness. Most of our DOING is fueled by some form of fear. We fear not having enough, so we get very busy doing things that will ensure that we always have enough. But no matter how much you have, the fear is still there. It's very subtle, but you've got to be willing to acknowledge that the fear is lurking underneath.

Many of us are so busy DOING that we don't take the time to stop and ask, WHY am I doing this? WHY am I rushing? WHY am I feeling stressed? This was evidenced to me in a conversation I had many years ago with a man called Derek. He had a lot of success as a businessman. The company he founded was thriving and he lived in a small mansion in a fashionable suburb of Dublin. He had a lovely family around him and his wife adored him. Perfect, you might think. He has it all. Eh, no! Scratch that! Even though he had 'achieved' what most of us would regard as 'success' he was always stressed. He was always anxious. He drank too much. He planned his future meticulously. When I expressed concern that he wasn't enjoying his life the way he could, he confided in me. "I'm full of fear all the time. My whole personality is based on being fearful about what might happen. I'm riddled with anxiety and worry, but I hide it by pretending. Nobody knows that my forceful personality and my drive to succeed are all coming from fear. I'm afraid to stop too. I don't know who I am, without all this striving and all this worrying. I'm afraid to let go. It's as if I need to control the future even though I know I can't, and I waste my life worrying about what might happen. I worry about my partner. I worry about my children too. I wish I could stop worrying, but I can't. I need a few drinks almost every night just to calm me down, to relax."

Who can wait quietly while the mud settles?
Who can remain still until the moment of action?
Observers of the Tao do not seek fulfilment.
Not seeking fulfilment, they are not swayed by desire for change.
– Tao Te Ching

Light

I remember a sunny day many years ago when I was driving in the Irish countryside with my four children in the back seat of the car. My eldest daughter, aged eight, spotted a rainbow and said, "Let's find the pot of gold at the end of the rainbow. It's just over there, Daddy, only a few fields away!" So, being a carefree and slightly spontaneous dad (sometimes!) I took the next turn right and we drove around for mile after mile while the kids shouted directions from the back of the car. "It's just over there... Take that lane way up on the left... Reverse back, quickly!... It moved!"

We had a lot of fun and of course we never quite got to claim the pot of gold! The rainbow wasn't 'real' in terms of the physical world, because it was just light and moisture, appearing as a rainbow of colors through an alchemical process. It looked like it was real and it looked like it kept moving away from us every time we'd get close. But even though you can see the rainbow, you cannot 'touch' the spectrum of light. It touches you. It touches the air. It touches the earth. It touches the water. It touches everything.

In the physical world the sun is our source of light. When the light of the sun hits water droplets, it refracts into a rainbow of seven colors and many gradients in between. Isaac Newton discovered this when he passed a beam of sunlight through a prism. When the light came out the other side it wasn't white anymore. It had spread into seven different colored rays: Red, Orange, Yellow, Green, Blue, Indigo and Violet. Newton called this "dispersion" – and he called the different colored rays the spectrum. He also saw that passing the rays back again through the prism turned them back into white light. His conclusion was that white light was made up of seven different colored rays, which are one part of the electromagnetic spectrum, those that are discernible to the human eye. There are lots of frequencies and colors in between these seven, and there are also some that we can't see (ultraviolet, infrared and so on).

We now know that the different colors in the rainbow all vibrate at different frequencies. Something similar is happening inside of us, because we also vibrate at different frequencies. Some days we just feel heavy. Other days we feel light and uplifted. Sometimes we even feel on fire! Science is beginning to understand all of this, and I'm convinced that, one day soon, we will scientifically prove that we are beings of light housed in physical bodies. In a strange way we are like the rainbow. When the light of consciousness enters into a body it refracts into seven planes (or energy vibrations). These are represented by the seven chakras, the data centers that receive, assimilate and distribute our energy. This is what Eastern medicine is based on. These chakras range from the physical all the way up to intuition and thought. In other words we are diffusion of the light of consciousness manifesting on different planes. We manifest as emotions, as creativity, as physical bodies, as intuition, as sexuality, as communication and thought. These are all the different 'colors' of consciousness which make up a human being.

I'm sure you've had an AHA! moment, when your perception shifts and you 'see' differently, or you just know something in a different way. It's as if light comes in and informs us that we've been blind. This often happens when we're in a really bad place in our lives, when the pain is so great that we suddenly break open. The old shatters, and the light can now get in. The reason we don't experience this more often is that the light of consciousness does not often penetrate us to the core. Our ego is in the way, like a hardened shell around us. Young children don't have fully developed egos, so they can operate from the deeper level of knowing quite naturally – if we let them. We can see this more clearly with an example.

A child walks into a room full of people. She's never met anyone in the room before and she's only five years old. She walks directly across the room and sits down beside an old man, puts her little hand on his arm, looks at him and speaks with her eyes. They say, "I understand. I know that you're sad. It's OK to cry." His eyes well up and he begins to cry. "How did you know?" he wonders.

The child picked up the old man's sadness at an energetic level the moment she walked into the room. This is something we can all do. I know. I've done some psychic training and been amazed at what I 'knew.' I was speaking to a friend of mine the other day, recounting one of my early experiences, when six or seven of us sat in a semicircle in a small room in Dublin. A woman we had never seen before came in and sat down in front of us, without saying a word. We were asked to 'read' her.

I was quite nervous but I found the courage to speak up when it got to my turn. One of the things I 'saw' was a young girl sailing in a small boat and an enclosed harbor, and I knew (intuitively) that I was seeing her childhood. At a later stage of my reading I became aware that the spirit of her maternal grandmother came 'into the room' and was present with us. Remember that the subject woman was not allowed to speak or give any visual clues or confirmation to us as we spoke. I was brave enough to mention the sailing, but to be honest, I was a bit freaked out by the dead grandmother! I was a beginner who hadn't learned to trust the deeper knowing, so I didn't mention it. We moved into silence again and then onto the next 'reader.' She spoke for a little while and then said: "Your grandmother on your mom's side has been in the room with us for a while too!"

Damn – I knew that! When we had all finished the volunteer spoke and said she had grown up in Dun Laoghaire, a coastal suburb of Dublin with a lovely harbor. She had sailed a lot as a child. So, my psychic reading was right in both cases, but I hadn't developed enough trust in my own intuition to say everything I saw and knew.

Listen up! Science can't explain everything. We are more than we think. We have to be, because we're touching into new possibilities every day. We're getting new ideas all the time. They come from somewhere. Get out of your programmed head and into some space. Slow down. Breathe. True creativity is birthed in the space between your thoughts, which is available to us any time we choose it. It's called consciousness.

But here's the difference between children and adults. The child knew what needed to be done and did it. Her body simply responded to her intuitive knowing. She walked over and put her hand in his because that's what was needed. Most adults, even if they somehow knew the man was grieving, would shy away from such immediate and direct contact with someone they didn't know. Why? Because fear gets in the way. Fear is what blocks the light of our consciousness. Our consciousness might know that the man needs to be reassured through a physical gesture, but somewhere on the journey from head to heart to body, our 'knowing' gets blocked. We become logical. We get sensible. We rationalize. We fear. We listen to the fearful voice that says something like, "Oh, what would people think?"

I remember a vivid scene many years ago, in a room full of people, at a workshop in Scotland. A very powerful woman was experiencing huge anger and was voicing it directly to the workshop leader. Usually I'm very quiet in large groups. That's my default position! But, while this was happening in front of my eyes, some deep knowing nudged me to stand up. To my amazement I found myself speaking and asking permission to approach her. I looked into her eyes, pointed to her heart and said some very simple words to her. Her anger evaporated and she began to experience deep healing tears. It wasn't 'me' that did anything. It was more that I surrendered to a call or a knowing. I allowed the light to come through.

However, most of us walk around disconnected from this inner light, or Christ self, or illumined consciousness, or realized self. The words don't really matter, but when we are disconnected from the light we are stuck in fear and separation, the primary foundations of the ego. Ego gets in the way.

Let's use an analogy. When light hits a physical object (let's say a stone) it produces a shadow behind the stone. Why? Because the stone is in the way and cannot be penetrated by light. In the same way our ego cannot be penetrated by the light because it sees itself as separate from the light. The ego wants to exist as a separate entity and does not want to die. In our egos we are very sure of who we are (a man, a teacher, a good person – and so on) and that's how we present ourselves to the world. It's very easy to have a fixed idea of 'who we are.'

But remember that light produces a shadow behind anything in its way and so your shadow is 'who you're not.' To be more accurate it's who you think you're not. When you are very sure of who you are (e.g. a good person) you tend to reject anything that is the opposite (e.g. a bad person) in others and in yourself. Rejecting what you find in yourself or in others builds even more disconnection. Many people are very attached to their idea of who they are and very sure of who they're not. Even if you have a positive self-image it's usually based on some measure of success in the outside world. But notice that self-image, even a positive one, is still an image. It's not you.

This is why people jump off bridges when they lose their business, or their partner, or something they are very attached to. They have built their whole sense of identity on the external world, and more particularly, on attachment. Without the measure of success in the material world, any ego-based identity will struggle. You can work really hard at making sure that you have lots of material things, so that people measure you as successful. If your ego-identity is based on 'having,' then you may find that you are very afraid of 'not having.' People who struggle with money and live in poverty are your shadow, reflected back at you. You will not like to be around people who are poor. You will gravitate towards people who are invested in maintaining their self-image at the same level as you maintain yours.

From a spiritual point of view, 'having' or 'not having' are just opposite poles within the sphere of abundance. Neither is more virtuous than the other. Both are ideas based on comparison, which is a formidable weapon of the ego and the world of opposites. You either have or you don't. You're right or wrong. He's better than him. He's more successful than you. She's not who she used to be. His father was a better man than he is, and so on. The ego loves comparison!

Yes, your ego will tell you that you need to have things, and that you need to hold onto things. Of course, there's nothing wrong with having – nothing at all. But having is not the same as having to have. Having is not the same as needing to have. It's not the same as defining your identity based on what you have. It's this very energy, of need, of grasping, of holding on, that keeps us from the simple joy of being. You 'need' money, possessions, the perfect relationship. You 'need' the future to be assured. You 'need' to know that everything is under control, your control!

I'm not saying that there's anything wrong with these wonderful things, not at all. But if you continue to create your relationships and abundance with an underlying 'needy' or 'grasping' or 'have to' energy, then you are still suffering. And then the ego plays its biggest trick. It tells you that this is untrue, that you DON'T create your own experience of suffering. It tells you that it's the world's fault or someone else's fault. Why would the ego do that? Because it takes your attention away from itself. Remember that the ego doesn't want to be seen. It wants to blame. It wants to deflect. It wants to deny that you have the power to create your own experience.

The ego's mantra is "What's in it for me?" How can I get more – whether it's more power or more money or more love, because ultimately the ego believes that you are 'not enough.' So you need more to 'complete' yourself, and of course, you never have enough. The belief that we need more infects everyone in our society, even the most 'powerful' and the most 'wealthy.' This is the lie that the ego, or the false self, spreads – that in some way we're all defective and that the way to cure that 'defect' is to have more. I should know, because I did this for years and years.

Despite what the ego will say, there is nothing wrong with you. But hey, wake up! That's only a thought. "There's something wrong with me" is only a thought. If you drop it, along with the other thought that you 'need' anything at all, what happens for you? Try it.

When I finally recognized my ego, I wrote a poem about it.

The Lie

I don't speak very often
Because I don't want You to know
That I exist.
It's wonderful, that you think
You're me – Because without that
I would die.
I'm glad – that you've given me
Your Soul – though you've forgotten what it is – by now.
I could whisper to you
that I suspect
I FEAR to be Loved
and, if I was Honest
(which I'm not)
I would tell you that
unconditional Love terrifies me
because then
you wouldn't need me
anymore.
I suspect that
I also NEED to be Loved –
and, if I was Courageous
(which I'm not)
I would ask you to
Unconditionally love me.
But I can't, because it's too Vulnerable
and I'm too Ashamed.
Or
is it that I'm too Proud?
to be Honest
about my Needs.
The real Truth in all of this
is that I Hate my Need
for Love,

And I Need my Hatred
for Love –
Because these two –
Opposites –
Keep me alive –
in You.

Even now, at this stage of my development, I recognize that a part of me can be heartless. This acceptance, in itself, brings heart to the situation, so that I become less heartless! When we acknowledge and accept those parts of us that we have denied, kept hidden, or are ashamed of, we become bigger. When we acknowledge and accept the conditioned self (ego and shadow) we become our true self. When we acknowledge and accept the small self, we become the big self. When we acknowledge and accept the surface self, we become more of the deep self. When we accept our own shadow, we become more light. Paradox – again and again!

This Native American legend explains it slightly differently:

An old Cherokee is teaching his grandson about life.

"A fight is going on inside me," he said to the boy.

"It is a terrible fight and it is between two wolves. One is evil – he is anger, envy, sorrow, regret, greed, arrogance, self-pity, guilt, resentment, inferiority, lies, false pride, superiority, and ego."

He continued,

"The other is good – he is joy, peace, love, hope, serenity, humility, kindness, benevolence, empathy, generosity, truth, compassion, and faith. The same fight is going on inside you – and inside every other person, too."

The grandson thought about it for a minute and then asked his grandfather,

"Which wolf will win?"

> The old Cherokee simply replied,
> "The one you feed."

Remember that. You are a divine, infinite creator who has made the choice to be here. You can choose to feed whichever wolf you like. While I agree with the analogy that we can feed our own greed and arrogance, self-pity and so on, I see the other attributes as already there within us. It's not so much that we need to feed the love, compassion and truth. We simply need to consciously surrender into them and to allow them to come to the surface. When you do this you begin to attract not what the ego wants, but what you actually are. Conscious surrender means that all you have to 'do' is simply to be, to let go, to allow, to trust, and to move into that deeper place that is connected and in tune with the power that creates worlds. That power is constantly giving, constantly expanding – and never looking for anything back.

> Even after all this time, the sun never says to the earth 'you owe me.'
> – Hafiz (Sufi poet)

When this internal ego-world is brought into the light of consciousness, it struggles. It will not want to be exposed, and so you will meet lots of resistance. But if you stick with it for awhile the ego will begin to soften, and your shadow will be more and more exposed. In the physical world, the closer the stone gets to the light the bigger the shadow appears. It's the same for us. As we move closer to accepting what's inside us – the lies, the secrets, the shame, the guilt, the fears and insecurities – the shadows are revealed more and more. Yes, it will feel like your world is falling apart sometimes. That's part of the process because your normal holding patterns will be revealed and dissolved. Your defenses and hardened mental structures will start to let go and it may feel very chaotic for a while. So it's not too wise to try to get too close to the light too soon. There's an organic process at work within you. You need to trust that. When we are letting go of our layers (like Shrek!) it's wise to allow time to integrate it all, so that we are stronger in our being the next time we take a step closer to the light.

Exercise

As always, please write spontaneously, without that pesky internal censor!

The one thing about me that I am ashamed of is

_____

_____

_____

The one thing that I'm afraid to own up to is

_____

_____

_____

If it wasn't so difficult for me I'd love to

_____

_____

_____

Let's go back now to the idea of the light shining. Hopefully, you've answered those questions honestly, so some light is shining through into what was previously dark and unacknowledged within you. In those areas where you've opened up, there is less defense and less resistance to the light of truth. If you were to look behind you (as in the analogy of the stone and the shadow) you would still see the outline of your shadow, but you would also notice some light here and there in the midst of the darkness. As you open up more and more, you will find that you are travelling 'lighter' in your life. You will have more energy than you had beforehand, because you are not hauling lots of 'baggage' around to do with the past. On top of that you don't need to invest any energy in keeping up a 'self-image.' You begin to feel the real benefits of this work. You don't carry 'psychological time' around with you. The aging process slows down, and you may even look younger than you did a few years back.

As you continue to open up to the light your ego dissolves even more. You begin to sense the light within you and you know yourself as this light more and more. It's a feeling like becoming transparent, where there is no 'you.' What there is, instead, is a wonderful sense of belonging, to something far more loving and intelligent than your mind can imagine. You sense that this 'something' is both inside you and also outside you, reflected back to you. You see beauty and meaning in your own life, and also in the life all around you. You notice things at a deeper level. You hear the birds singing in a way you never did before. You feel strangely empty and full at the same time. You belong to yourself. You have come home.

Chapter 14

Naked, Innocent and Open

I was like a boy playing on the sea-shore, and diverting myself now and then finding a smoother pebble or a prettier shell than ordinary, whilst the great ocean of truth lay all undiscovered before me.
– Isaac Newton

I walked out the front door of our semi-detached house in the suburbs of Dublin and strolled down a few doors to call for my girlfriend. When I got to the right house, I rang the doorbell. A few seconds later, a woman in her late 30s answered the door, her eyes jumping out of their sockets at the sight of me! Before she could speak, I asked, "Is Eileen in?" "Yes," said the woman, and recovered her composure a little, "but I think you should go home first and put some clothes on." "Oh, OK," I said, "I'll come back in a few minutes." Yes, I had no clothes on. No, I wasn't embarrassed! Still naked, I walked back home. And no, I don't have a strange fetish for calling naked at people's front doors!

I'm glad to report that I was only four years old, and deliciously innocent. I hadn't yet experienced shame. I simply had no idea that there could be anything wrong with this. I suppose I saw naked animals everywhere, from cats and dogs to squirrels, cows and sheep. Animals don't feel shame, because it's a mind-made concept. My mind had yet to be programmed to tell me stories about my body. I simply had a body and I lived in it! It really was delicious. Like most young children I was fascinated and curious about my physical presence. But I didn't know shame.

Ah sure, no harm, them were the days, the 1960s and 70s in Dublin. Grey weather, grey smog from all the fireplaces churning out smoke, before the days of gas and oil central heating. Grey buildings, grey roads and grey houses. Those days we only had two shades of grey, not fifty. Plain old right and wrong. Our street was grey too, except for the long streak of black tar down the middle and the green grass verges on both sides. On hot summer days the tar would melt and we children would all pick at it, the way you'd pick at a scab on your arm. We'd form the tar into little balls and throw it at the grey garden walls, to make strange patterns and shapes. It was just a bit of fun, not really a sin. More like a prank, that's what we told ourselves. We didn't like to sin, 'cos it made you feel yucky inside and then you'd have to tell the priest about it. That wasn't much fun, no siree, not much fun at all, because we was all really scared of that confessional box. It reminded me of a stand-up coffin.

The priests had a way of making you feel even worse about your sins. Fr. Martin seemed especially interested in our sins. As we got older, we'd tell him stuff about kissin' and maybe feelin' the girls up and how good it felt. He'd ask questions about the girls and boys and what we all got up to. Then he'd tell us how bold we were and how we'd have to do penance. If I was into corporate speak I'd call it a win-win situation – we got absolved and the priest got kinda horny in the dark!

But when I was a young boy, I was scared of the dark and the priest and the whole God-is-watching-you thing. You couldn't see much in the confessional box but you could sure feel a whole lot! The unholy Trinity of guilt and fear and shame. Once I was so nervous I peed quietly while on my knees, a wee trickle of a sin. When the priest was finished absoluting me, I scampered quick as I could, not stopping for my three Hail Marys and how's your Father. As I left the church I glanced over my shoulder to look at the spidery and wrinkly old woman after me. Her knees would soon be feeling the warm caress of my sinful trickle.

Fast-forward a few years, when a 12-year-old boy had a stirring in his trousers. Nobody prepared me for my first erection, a statement that is probably true for most boys. I mean, how do you prepare for something like that? Who prepares you? Certainly not your mother... your father? Unlikely. A big brother? Perhaps, but in the kind of way that made you feel less than him. A teacher? Never. Sex education hadn't been invented yet. Perhaps the local priest? Er, hello! I drifted into the teenage years and the testosterone came with it, hard and urgent. My innocence was receding as fast as my Uncle Tom's hairline. He was a part-time artist who played a huge French horn, but I never knew why they called it French. We made up lots of jokes about horns and frenchies and blowing hard, because we couldn't say penises and condoms and fellatio. Those words hadn't arrived yet in Catholic Ireland. It was still only 1970.

Adults spoke about the body in ways that influenced my thinking about it. Irish Society seemed to believe that there was something sinful about having a body, let alone playing with your penis in the bath, as all young boys do. I remember feeling even more confused when the teenage years arrived. Hormones took over, hair sprouted in secret places, and lusty thoughts began to force themselves into my mind. At this stage my body was designed to have daily if not hourly erections, which is all very natural. The problem was that my mind had been conditioned to believe there was something shameful about that. You were not to talk about erections. You were not allowed to touch your genitals, and you were absolutely forbidden to take any pleasure in your sexuality. Sex was for procreation only. It was almost comical, except it wasn't. It was quite damaging for all of us who grew up in that era.

At fifteen years of age, lying down in my bed, I'd be erect within seconds. The inner conflict would flare up. "Don't touch it," said my conditioned Catholic mind, while my body screamed out for pleasure. "Resist the temptation" was in one corner of the ring, a hard and judgmental opponent. In the other corner my earthy sensual self danced around naked, singing a little ditty... "Your penis was made for love, your penis was made for love, touch it, touch it, touch it now." Well, not really, but you get the picture.

And so the battle would begin. It usually didn't last long though, and I would end up masturbating, despite the Catholic shame. Afterwards the guilt would creep in. There was no one to talk to about things like that and so most people walked around harboring their dirty little secrets. Sure, most people had sex and masturbated, including the priests in their cassocks and collars, but nobody talked about it. It was all hidden away in the shadows.

This kind of inner conflict produces what we call an energy block in your body, where two opposing forces meet. Each time the battle recommenced, the opponents would square up to each other. The hard and judgmental belief system versus the earthy sexuality. Even though the sexual urge won out almost every time, I could not fully enjoy the act itself without some level of shame at the time, and a large helping of guilt afterwards. So this energy block built and built in me every time my mind denied the truth of my body. Shame lodged inside me. I could feel it in my upper chest and face, like a hidden blush. The churches who condemned our sexuality have a lot to answer for, as they caused us to go to war with the natural sacredness of our bodies and our sexuality. I understand now that they needed us to believe we were sinners and that we needed redemption, and of course, that the only redemption came through them. Clever!

The majority of Catholics, priests included, felt huge shame around their sexuality as they tried hard to be 'good Christians.' I know of quite a few priests who were lucky enough to find women that loved them and loved their bodies, but that was all in secret. Some fought their urges desperately, trying to be 'good' – until their deeply repressed sexuality burst out in horribly damaging ways. It is incredible how much child abuse was going on and how it remained hidden for so long. It led to an organization called One in Four being founded in Ireland, and the name itself tells you the scale of the problem. It left an indelible mark on thousands of children. The church totally misunderstood that our bodies are vessels of spirit and that, therefore, our bodies are sacred vessels to be treasured and loved.

In my late teens, and still a virgin, I met the girl who would be my wife for a long time. Almost twenty years later, we split up. For the following year, I stayed deliberately single, having decided that I was too emotionally needy to enter into any relationship. I steered clear of the dating scene altogether, knowing that it would have been very easy to bury my pain by jumping into a relationship, something I had almost done when my marriage was going through its final death spasms. When your relationship is causing you a lot of pain, it's very easy to develop an unhealthy obsession with someone outside the relationship. You think it's love, but it's not. It's very intense, and you can't get it out of your mind. It's an emotional roller coaster, and you can easily get hooked on the ride. But, after a short time, the roller coaster stops and the intensity dwindles. On one level you realize you've been an idiot. On another level you want the intense feelings again. But it was never love. Love isn't always intense. Love isn't something you obsess about. Love is calmer, more ordinary, more honest and challenging than that.

Diary Transcript – April 2002

I feel very lonely, as if I'm disconnected from the whole world, as if nothing matters anymore, as if I don't matter. If I disappeared from the world who would care? I feel like 'breaking out' or getting very drunk and numbing this pain somehow. Rejection came at me again over and over, on Tuesday night. It was like the word REJECTION was being beamed in massive letters out of the sky – directly at me.

At the moment I don't feel loved by anyone. I feel very needy – like I want to cry my eyes out like a little child. I need someone to take care of me for a change. I need some hope, and I need to be told it's OK. I also feel like chucking in my job, and letting go of all the responsibility. I feel like making a big mistake for a change, maybe go on the drink big-time. Maybe I do need to let go and actually make some mistakes. I'm pissed off with being blamed for stuff I didn't actually do.

My need for a female touch and love is still there, although not as strong as it was. On one hand I long for a new relationship and on the other hand I'm fearful of a new relationship. I think I'll also feel guilty if I do get involved with someone else. I still feel married and I can't take off my ring yet, and yet I'm so sure that I don't want to rekindle the relationship.

So where is the guilt coming from? We've been separated for almost a year now. The fear is easy to understand, it's my fear of making a mess of a relationship again. But the guilt? What's all that about? I also felt very happy for a while last week and I ended up feeling guilty about that too! My marriage broke up a year ago and here I am feeling guilty about feeling happy! As I see it, I am taking responsibility for somebody else's emotions, again. I have to learn to stop doing that. I'm not responsible for how somebody else feels if I'm not deliberately hurting them.

The healing work I was doing had opened up my heart, but what next? There's a common misconception out there, that real men know what they want and that they will go after it until they get it. Eh, no!

I had no idea what I wanted, so that one is definitely a myth. A lot of men don't know what they want. They have no idea. Some simply love the chase and most women love to be chased. Men love to play games, but Xboxes and Wiis are nothing compared to the highs and lows of the chasing and dating game. By the time I got to even contemplate dipping my toes into the relationship world, the rules had changed. Twenty years on, it wasn't as simple as it had been. 'Birds' had evolved into chicks and peacocks. Some women had taken an evolutionary leap to become cougars, pumas and jaguars – all preying on younger men. Older men who liked younger women were known as cheetahs, though you have to be careful how you pronounce this one! A friend of mine told me to watch out for hyenas too – yikes! It was a brave New World for me.

Thankfully I expanded my own comfort zones, and later on, in my forties, I had some beautiful sexual and intimate experiences which would have shocked the former me. To get to that point, however, I had some internal restructuring to do. It's a funny thing when you realize that you have some fears that you didn't know about, until you did. Yes, I know, it's kinda hard to put into words. It's similar to the moment when you know that you don't know as much as you thought you knew! About life. About relationships. About yourself. Suddenly the circumstances you find yourself in expand the world you knew and inhabited, and a new you grows into that expanded space. It's not always easy to allow yourself to grow into the new you, because it's got that heady mixture of fear and excitement in it. We often come to choice points where we can allow the fear to keep us stuck, or burn through it and grow.

What I decided was that I needed some socially easy way to be around single women, and so I plucked up the courage to enroll in salsa classes. There I was, tentative and unsure of myself, forty-two years of age but feeling like an awkward 15 year old! It felt strangely intimate to be holding a woman's hand, another arm across her shoulders, our faces only a few inches from each other at times. It was illogical to feel slightly guilty too – I had been separated for a year now! But I moved my body to the music and I began. Straightaway the teacher pointed out that a few of us men needed to loosen up around the hips! Of course, she meant me, didn't she? My face flushed as my eyes stayed glued to the bellies and hips that swayed and pulsed their way around the room. "Come on, guys, swivel those hips. Make shapes with those buttocks. Exaggerate if you have to!" It was the complete antithesis to the Irish dancing I had learned as a child, where your hips stayed frozen solid, but your arms and legs moved frantically! However, my saving grace was that I loved music. That pushed me through my fears of physical closeness to women I didn't know. As the weeks went on I settled in to this new community of dancers, and I began to experience a sense of freedom in my body. My frozen hips began to thaw! Six months later, the whole group went away to a hotel for a full weekend's dancing. On the first night I ended up at an impromptu party where the drink was flowing freely, and we danced until 3am. I woke up on the Saturday morning in someone else's bed. My initiation was complete.

A few months later I discovered a different form of dancing. A friend of mine had recommended something called 5Rhythms dancing, a sort of moving meditation. There was a two-hour evening class every week in an old school hall, at 7pm on Sunday, and I decided to go along, on my own. I was a little late, and tentatively opened the door into the hall. Music, trance-like and rhythmic, was pumping out of two black speakers up on a stage. Some people were limbering up and stretching, while others looked like they were trying out a new form of horizontal dancing, writhing and pulsing on the floor in slow motion. Another ten or so were swaying and twisting around the hall, each one in their own little bubble. A bald young man with a long straggly beard was hopping on one foot incessantly, while a low hum came from his lips. I did that quick double-take thing, where you wonder, just for a second, if you're dreaming, and a ten-foot giant will burst through from the darkness backstage. Eh, no. Apparently I wasn't dreaming, and to my own surprise, I didn't hightail it out the door. I stayed and I'm so glad I did.

5Rhythms was created by an amazing lady called Gabrielle

Roth. Here's how Wiki explains it:

> The practice of the five rhythms is said by Gabrielle Roth to put the body in motion in order to still the mind. The five rhythms (in order) are flowing, staccato, chaos, lyrical, and stillness. The five rhythms, when danced in sequence, are known as a "Wave."

This movement was incredibly liberating for my body and soul.

5Rhythms led me to explore my breath and body awareness, my connection to others and my self-expression. It touched into my body in ways that astounded me, opening up deeply held fears and wounds. It taught me new concepts of containment, emotional fluidity and deep stillness. I danced a two-hour Wave almost every week for a few years, sharing a live collective experience with an ever-changing group of people, guided by a facilitator/DJ. At times it was a tremendously exhilarating experience, particularly at peak moments when I lost myself in the group energy, somewhat like a rave without the drugs! The group experience allows you to make connections and share magical moments with other dancers, without even speaking. Your body does all the talking, as you're often invited to move and dance with a partner, or within small groups of three or four. This opened up new and unexpected vistas for me, meeting each person's rhythm and energy with mine. As I danced my way through weekends and weeklong residential workshops I learned to bring everything I was feeling into the dance and to allow my body to express what it needed to express. Some dances found me shy and insecure, others wild and carefree. At times I flirted outrageously and other times I just wanted to be left alone. I felt expansive, closed, free, tight, gentle, strong, empathic, cold, superior, inferior, powerful, vulnerable, ecstatic, calm, connected, separate. You name it, I felt it.

When you allow your body to feel what's going on, to let go

and do exactly what it wants, your Internal Censor and Inner Critic show up a lot. Your mind gets very active at the beginning.

"What age do you think you are, spinning around on the floor?... That's not dignified, especially as there's four of you now... Stand up!... You look ridiculous, swaying there with your arms stretched out as if in prayer – this is not a church, for God's sake!... Yes, she's very sexy but she's out of your league... Dancing back to back, what are you like, and with a guy?... You're the worst dancer in here, look at her, she's so graceful compared to you... You're like a tiger pacing up and down in a cage."

That last one was revelation for me. I WAS pacing up and down, covering the same ten meters or so over and over again, backwards and forwards. My body was trying to tell me something – that it, and therefore I, felt caged, imprisoned in some way. As I kept moving it came to me. It was my anger, caged inside me. It wanted to get out. These are the kind of revelations that kept happening to me during my four or five years of dancing the 5Rhythms. I found myself breaking through energetic restrictions that I held deep in the body – restrictions that I didn't even know were there. Some of them kept a lid on my spontaneity. Some of them kept a lid on my anger, my sadness, my frustration, my self-loathing, my grief. At times I ended up crying soft tears of release. Other times my whole body was shaking with energy and ecstasy. Sometimes all I could do was a slow Indian hand dance while the rest of me was raging or weeping. We weren't supposed to stop moving, according to the facilitator. Keep moving, and keep on allowing whatever is happening. It was an important lesson, and it taught me that I can still be present even when my emotions want to overwhelm me.

That's something most of us are not used to doing. We either suppress the emotion or it takes us over so that we fall into some kind of drama. We don't know how to be with our emotions and still engage with life. I call it dual attention. One part of you stays grounded and present as you watch the other part of you exploding with whatever emotion is moving through. In 5Rhythms, all the emotions are processed in the dance. It's like watching the drama of your past unfolding through your body. You don't censor. You don't hold back or hold in or hold on. Everything goes into the dance until your body arrives at the Stillness part of the practice. In this last Rhythm I often experienced sublime ecstasy, deep peace and a strong connectedness to the sacred. Years later I discovered a writing practice that has the same end result, where you allow the words to flow onto the page, without censorship, without neat lines or respect for margins. Everything flows out into the words, and eventually you're left with an incredible sense of space and peace inside. In her wonderful book *Writing Down the Bones*, Natalie Goldberg calls it "putting all your drama on the page."

They're just two of the ways I have discovered to help me "empty out" – as the Buddhists put it. If you're a Christian, it's akin to emptying all the old wine first. Let Go, and Let God. Once you've done that, there's a lot of space inside and you can fill up with new wine. Mine's a cabernet!

Fast-forward a few years, and I am in my mid-forties now, driving west across Ireland. I'm leaving the suburban sprawl of Dublin and all my responsibilities behind. I need this weekend away. I need to shed all of my roles for a while, so I can see who I am without them all. Father. Provider. Businessman. Director. Single Separated Parent. Spiritual Seeker. Bloody idiot sometimes!

I am visiting a female friend in Galway, partly because I don't have many male friends. I'm at a stage where I don't have any real interest in the male-dominated business world anymore. A weekend away with a group of men playing golf, drinking heavily, and whatever else you're having, is my worst nightmare. I just don't cut it in that world anymore. In my new world, I'm sad to say, men are hugely in the minority. That means that I have a lot of platonic female friends. The woman I'm visiting is ten years younger than me, a real free spirit with a big Spanish heart, and I'm looking forward to spending the weekend at her place.

I arrive in darkness. She answers the door in an off-the-shoulder blouse, cut-off jeans and sandals. Her hair is brushed to one side, and her eyes radiate a warm welcome. The soft pink lipstick is a lovely contrast to her dark skin and round brown eyes. She says, "Hola, Eoin," and wraps her arms around me, as she always does. We stay there, bodies pressed against each other for a long time, but then again, all of this is normal behavior for us. She greets most men like this and I'm the same with any woman who is comfortable with a full body welcome. Some things do change!

A while ago I began to observe people hugging each other.

First are the "Neck-up Huggers." Their necks may touch, they may blow a kiss or two, and that's it. No chests, breasts or tummies meet. It's perfunctory and pretty sterile stuff.

Second are what I call the "Slap-dash Huggers." Most men are in this category. There's a loud greeting, a handshake, and a very quick thump or two on the back, followed by a quick dash back to safety! SLAP – and DASH!

Category Three are the "Waist-up Huggers." Your body meets theirs from the waist up. You can smell their perfume (or sweat!) and you can feel the rise and fall of their breathing. Family members often fit in this category. Both parties make sure there's plenty of space between the body parts below the waist. Genitals do not say hello to each other!

Last are the "Full-Body Huggers." No holding back. Safe. Warm. Bodies fully present. Stay as long as it feels right. I've stayed in full-body hugs with many women for three to five minutes and longer, simply breathing and enjoying the closeness and the intimacy of it. It's not sexual but it is sensual. It's inclusive and welcoming. There is a difference.

Right now with Sonia, she is doing something down there. Yes, down there. We're about two minutes into our full-body hug and she starts to move and press her hips into mine. This is unusual and I can feel the energy shifting from sensual to sexual. Grinding against me? Not quite, but you get the idea. I don't want this right now, although my erection seems to say otherwise. That's one of the issues of being a man. We can pop up at the worst possible time – and we often do!

As I pull back and out of the hug I'm suddenly aware of an unconscious fear I've been carrying. It's about women who come on to me. I'm afraid of them, but why? What's the big deal? They want me, and a part of me enjoys that. But I somehow seem to magnify it into meaning more than it is, even though I'm at the stage where I am very comfortable with my sexuality. I've done my fair share of Mantra and Tantra, or "Chanting and Panting" as some people put it! So what's going on? I begin to uncover a fear-based belief that has been hanging around in my psyche for quite some time. My train of thought went something like this – "If a woman wants sex, she will want something else too. After sex, you're in a relationship. Aren't you? Relationship means that you have to spend more time with this woman. Don't you? It means you're not free anymore. Ouch! It means that she owns a part of you, in some strange way. Double ouch! She gets to set some of the rules. You can't look at another woman. You can't talk about ex-girlfriends, let alone spend time with them. Actually you've got to stop seeing them. You're with me now!"

All of this programming and belief was coming to the surface as I gently eased my body out of the hug, and we settled in to have a bite to eat. After dinner I took a shower, and as the water hammered at my body, I decided to talk about my fears to Sonia if she was open to it. When I finished, I dried myself quickly and shrugged my body into jeans and a clean white shirt. Shoes were unnecessary in this house, with its variety of soft rugs and Indian tapestries covering most of the floor area.

"Fancy a chat?" I asked when I came back to the lounge. "There's something I'd like some help with."

"Sure," she said, "what's up?"

I told her that I was afraid that she was coming on to me. She flicked her hair.

"Coming on to you? I was!" she said – "And so what?"

No games here. I loved her honesty. We began to talk. She was the first woman I ever spoke to in depth about sex, love and relationship. About sex without love. About relationship without sex. About sex just for the sake of it. What it was like for a woman to have sex, physically and emotionally. What she liked and what she didn't. What I liked and what I didn't. We swapped stories all night, nestled on the couch, sipping a strong red wine. We talked about the pressure on women to look a certain way, what it was like to be ashamed of your body. What was like to physically open up to your partner and allow yourself to be penetrated. How that felt for a man too, in a deeply loving relationship, and how different it was to have sex when you didn't want to, when your body wasn't ready. We spoke about how our bodies loved to be held and stroked and touched, mine included.

As we opened up to each other, something in me shifted and loosened, though I suppose the wine helped! I told her about my Catholic upbringing, and how, when I met my wife-to-be at 20 years of age, I was still a virgin. I told her that more than twenty years later I had found myself single again, with no experience outside the marriage bed.

Now, a few years further on, I was still discovering and unearthing my beliefs about women, sex and relationships. I spoke to her about things I had always been ashamed to talk about. It's not something that comes naturally to the male of the species, to talk openly about our feelings. We seem to be hardwired differently, as if being closed and guarded means being strong, and that being open and vulnerable means being weak. I was learning to challenge those ancestral beliefs in myself, and I loved the inner freedom that it gave me.

I also spoke to her about not being 'The One,' and that I wasn't ready for a committed relationship. She laughed. "Sex with me doesn't mean that I have to be 'The One' or that I want something more from you. I know that you're not The One for me either, but we both enjoy being with each other. Having sex doesn't mean that our enjoyment or companionship has to stop, or change in any way." That was a bit of an epiphany for me. I realized how closed I was to the possibility of enjoying sex and intimacy without any unspoken agenda or additional meaning. A woman could enjoy being with me without wanting anything from me. Phew!

We moved on to talk about touch in all of its forms – and yes, we practiced! Soft single finger strokes from neck to buttocks. Sweeping and circling motions around the base of the spine. Gentle nail-scraping across the shoulders. Strong upward strokes from the knees to the belly. We practiced heart connection, eye connection and how to sense into what felt right. We practiced touching without any agenda, because we had agreed that there would be no genital stimulation at that time. It opened up a new depth in me, and a deeper trust of the feminine.

When I left on Sunday I felt something huge had shifted, and I am forever grateful to Sonia. I had learned something really important. Opening into fear leads to freedom. I had learned that fear isn't ultimately real because it disappears once you get into it. This learning served me well as I explored more and more deeply, getting increasingly comfortable about being open. About six months later, I found myself at another choice point during a workshop I attended high up in the mountains of Scotland, where I was one of three men in a group of about thirty women. We had spent the morning invoking and sensing into the powerful loving energy of the Divine Feminine. It's a phrase that I was becoming very accustomed to although some part of me was afraid of how powerful it was. At one stage I found myself speaking up openly in front of the group.

"I have something to work on," I said to the workshop leader, "but I'm not quite sure how to put it into words." "How does it feel?" he asked. At this stage in my journey I was well used to diving into my feelings, sensing where they were in my body and talking about what I found there. "Well," I said, "I'm sitting here surrounded by so many beautiful women who have shown me what it's like to deeply embody the feminine. I can feel the depth of the feminine love in this room, but I can't fully connect with it. I seem to have some fear of really opening up to it, even though on a surface level it looks like I'm very comfortable. It's as if I can allow love, but on my terms. It feels like I'm still holding back."

"Where do you feel that holding back?" "In my chest," I answered, "it feels like I have some deep fear of letting the love all the way into my heart." I was asked to come into the center of the room and to lie down on my back with my eyes closed. I felt scared and exposed, not knowing what might happen next. At this point the facilitator said a prayer and invited anyone who wanted to help to come into the center and place their hands on me. My eyes remained closed as my body began to register the warmth of all the hands that were placed on me. My senses were heightened, and my whole body felt very warm. Then the next level of prayer and invocation began. I fell into what seemed like a trance, as if I was surrounded by angels, and every palm print and finger pressure on my body was a point of light, gradually opening up the hardness in my body. I began to weep quietly. It grew into a sobbing as my whole body began to convulse. More prayer and invocation, and while I don't remember the actual words, it was something like: "Great Spirit, please use the outstretched arms and hands of all these Goddesses to pour love into the body of this man, and to soften and release any pain that he is holding in or holding onto. Go deep into his muscles, his muscle memory, his ligaments, bones and bone marrow, into his blood, into the cellular memory of any sense of abandonment, loss or grief, and replace it all with the light and love of the divine feminine as it is embodied by these women." Words cannot really describe the depths of what happened to me on the floor, but I had finally opened up to love and experienced deep healing of all the parts of me that were not able to receive love. I felt incredibly open. I felt a deep space within me that wasn't there before. There's an old Zen story that captures this very well:

Once, a long time ago, there was a wise Zen master. People from far and near would seek his counsel and ask for his wisdom. Many would come and ask him to teach them, enlighten them in the way of Zen. He seldom turned any away.

One day an important man, a man used to command and obedience, came to visit the master. "I have come today to ask you to teach me about Zen. Open my mind to enlightenment." The tone of the important man's voice was one used to getting his own way.

The Zen master smiled and said that they should discuss the matter over a cup of tea. When the tea was served the master poured his visitor a cup. He poured and he poured and the tea rose to the rim and began to spill over the table and finally onto the robes of the wealthy man. Finally the visitor shouted, "Enough. You are spilling the tea all over. Can't you see the cup is full?"

The master stopped pouring and smiled at his guest. "You are like this tea cup, so full that nothing more can be added. Come back to me when the cup is empty. Come back to me with an empty mind."

In order to transform, we must empty ourselves of all that is not love. We must open up our hearts, our bodies and our minds, and surrender to the feminine aspect, the love and nurturing that wants to heal our disconnection. I often think it's more difficult for us men to surrender and let go. Most of us have defined masculinity in terms of being tough or rigid, and that's understandable given the history of mankind. As I walk around Dublin and Belfast, I see so many men whose bodies and faces are closed, hardened, wounded, fearful, angry, disconnected. Yes, I see it in women too although they seem to have a more natural inclination towards inclusion, empathy and openness.

One of the practices that helped me to open up and reveal myself to myself was writing. This book is probably a natural result of the writing muscle I have been using on and off for the last twenty years. During the last years of marriage I kept a special notebook where I wrote down anything at all, how I felt, what I was thinking, and so on. The delicious part of it was that it was uncensored – because I was beginning to understand that 'I' was not my thoughts or feelings. So they came and they went, thoughts and feelings, some of them crazy, spiteful, pain-filled, resentful and judgmental. I could see that they were just passing through me and that the very act of writing them down gave them less power over me – but unfortunately my ex-wife didn't agree with my metaphysical concepts! One day, she decided to read my explicitly private journal. My fatal mistake may have been DO NOT READ! printed large and loud on the front. Who could resist taking a peek?

The outcome of all of that wasn't very pretty, and we both awakened a lot of anger – me, over my boundary being crossed, and she, because of what I had written. Most of us in relationship don't really want to know what the other thinks and feels all the time, because, unless we're very evolved, we'll make it mean something about ourselves. We're used to hiding what's really going on, but we don't realize how damaging that is, to ourselves and those we love. I guess that if we all told our partners every crazy thought we have, the police or the men in the white coats would be called in, and we'd be taken away!

At this stage of my life, I was understanding how important it was for me not to hide myself, psychologically, emotionally or physically. There's a delicious freedom in it, being nakedly yourself. There is a release in it too, letting go of fears, of shame and of pretense. Miranda MacPherson, a wonderful teacher that I've done some work with, uses the term "undefended." Rather than waste our energy in 'defending,' we free ourselves up, by recognizing and dropping our defenses. It's a process that takes a long time, and leads you into a deep and unshakeable trust.

About a year after beginning to write on a regular basis, I attended another weeklong workshop. It was called something like "Embracing the Light" – and it was the kind of work that allowed us to go deep into our spontaneous and natural selves. The fifth day found most of the 25 participants, mainly women, invoking the Divine Feminine. Our prayer was that our spirits would feel completely at home in our bodies. As we walked and moved around the room to some powerful music, a beautiful and enveloping presence began to flood the room, and people began to spontaneously remove their clothing. We swayed and danced as more and more of us stripped off all of our clothes, no matter what age or body shape. It is difficult for people who have not experienced Spirit moving through them to understand this type of experience. Most will see it as something that it was not. For me, it was an incredibly sacred and liberating experience, and I am eternally grateful to the men and women who were brave enough to reveal their inner beauty and allow their radiance to shine unashamedly.

Integrating our spirituality with our earthy and sexual nature helps to unlock any mental and emotional shame we may carry around our sexuality. Conversely, integrating our sexual consciousness with our spiritual nature will help to ground it, to make it more real and accessible to us as we live our daily lives.

All of my experiences had opened me up to connecting more deeply with my body, and I found myself simply wanting to be naked more often, wandering out into the back garden of my suburban home after dark, allowing the warm summer breeze to brush my hair and caress my skin. One particular morning I wandered naked through a local forest, feeling incredibly earthy, connected to the land and the trees, but keeping a watchful eye out for humans! Come on, most of you have done some frolicking in the woods – or if you haven't, you'd like to!

Chapter 15

Relationship and Manifestation

"It helps if you remember that everyone is doing their best from their level of consciousness."
– Deepak Chopra

When it comes to relationships, I'm always amazed at how vague we can be. I ask clients who are looking for love:
"So, what is it you want?"
"Well, I just want a relationship."
"A relationship," I say. "With a horse?"
They usually laugh.
"No, of course not. With a man."
"Oh, I see," I say. "A relationship with a ninety-year-old man who drinks beer all day, is ten stone (140 lbs.) overweight and misogynistic?"
They laugh again. "No, of course not."
"OK, so what EXACTLY do you want?"
A nervous laugh. "To be honest, I don't know. I haven't given it much thought."

No wonder we keep attracting the wrong type of person into our lives! We put so much effort into choosing a new outfit or a new house, but we're often very vague when it comes to the relationship we want. We've got to be very clear about what we want to attract.

Before I met Jenny, I had been very clear about what type of woman I wanted to meet, and the type of relationship I wanted. I spent some time writing it all out, and sensing into how it would feel to be in that type of relationship. Whenever I met someone and went out for a few dates, I was able to run through my internal checklist to see if we were a match. Whether you believe in the Law of Attraction or not, it makes complete sense to me to work out and know what I want. Once I had done that, I decided to put my 'specifications' up on a dating Web site. I didn't want to waste time messaging and meeting women who didn't fit my vision. Scanning through people's profiles tells you a lot about them.

> I enjoy meeting new people and going to new places. I love the outdoors, watching movies, dancing, and traveling. A great date can be staying at home with a movie and popcorn, or a night on the town. Well, that is a little about me, if you are interested say hello and we will chat.

That's the type of bland generic profile that tells you nothing. I don't know why people go through all the rigmarole of filling in all those questionnaires and then post a profile that is generic, boring, and full of clichés like: "I am as comfortable staying in as staying out!"
Here's what I posted about me:

> I am still enjoying 'the journey' – and very much into spiritual expansion and personal growth. I love a challenge! I am a deep thinker, articulate, considerate, wise and foolish at the same time:) I look after myself well and I have a serious and a wacky side to me :) While I'm not into the clubbing/drinking scene, I do love to dance, and also enjoy walking, meditation and exercise. I look and feel a lot younger than my age, I'm solvent and self-sufficient – and I don't need a Mammy! But I would enjoy meeting someone I can get to know slowly, and maybe really click with on all levels... I am an eternal optimist!

There was a section to describe your ideal partner too, and mine read like this:

My ideal partner would be... sure of herself in this world, committed to whatever she is passionate about, able to really connect and be honest, spiritually aware, wanting a depth of connection beyond the norm. I would like to meet a woman who is comfortable with her femininity, both physically and emotionally grounded, and aware of and sensitive to all of life. A big heart, a high level of consciousness and a desire to grow in awareness together are essential – otherwise don't waste your time messaging me please. And last but not least, she's got to be able to have a good laugh at herself – and me!

While I didn't meet the love of my life through the dating Web site, it helped me to get very clear on what I wanted. I met quite a few women, had some great times and kept noticing what I didn't want. That helped me to constantly refine what it was I did want. I was not going to stay with someone unless I knew, deep in my belly, that she was right for me in every way. My own experience of relationship had led me to understand that we always know what's right for us and what's not. We arrive at that point where we know it's time for change, but fear holds us back. Most of us know what it's like to run into the arms of something fuzzy and warm, and what its appeal is, but we also know what it's like to stay in something that is not good for either party. What we need is the ability to discern our own truth while noticing if any part of our decision is still influenced by duty, guilt or fear. Feeling into and discerning our deeper truth within that wider context is an act of the spiritually mature, and is not something that we're necessarily used to doing. It becomes a 'skill' that grows as we use it – I certainly didn't possess it in my first 40 years on the planet!

Six months after I became very clear on what I wanted, I hopped on a plane to Italy. It was there, on a hill, that I met the lovely Jenny, who is now my best friend, confidante, business partner, lover and soulmate. We are passionately committed to conscious growth in our relationship, physically, mentally, emotionally and spiritually. When growth stops, which it has for a few months now and then, we know that something is 'off,' and that we need to talk about what's not working. Without growth we aren't fulfilling the purpose of relationship. Real growth means that we explore our edges, our wounds and our fears in relation to anything that comes up. We are wise enough to know that this level of intimacy will trigger any unhealed parts of us, whether that's subtle fears, abandonment, rejection, control, you name it. As we become clearer and clearer about our part in the dysfunction of previous relationships, we create a new way of relating. It means that our relationship feels very alive. Yes, it can be a little scary too, because it means that growth and honesty come first, even at the expense of the relationship!

It means that we can talk about anything – ex-partners, sexual preferences, what's working for us and what's not, whether we'd like some space from the other for a few days, how to express our anger without making it about the other, how to say what we need without it being a demand, and so on. We can express how we feel, talk about our fantasies, reveal our secrets. It's something akin to "radical honesty" – a phrase coined by Brad Blanton. If you really want to know someone, let them be honest with you and don't react! That's the hard part, because when someone is completely honest with you, it will trigger you. As you work through your own triggers and defenses, you'll both experience what it's like to be truly known and seen. And that, my friends, is real love, crazy love, blissful ecstatic love, where nothing is hidden.

If a relationship is not growing, it will stagnate. Thankfully, I now embrace growth and change and, as a result, our relationship has deepened immensely. I can honestly say that, here now in 2016, I love this woman more deeply and comprehensively than I thought possible. And she loves me equally, if not more fiercely.

It's very different to how I used to see relationship and what it meant. For many of us, we seem to reach a point where we want things to stay the same. We want our partners to stay the same and they want us to be a certain way too. We get very comfortable with the sameness, but there's no real juice in it anymore. Once we establish these norms of expectation, we tend to repress our true selves in order to please the other and so we build up a storehouse of unexpressed emotions. We don't grow at all. In fact, we stagnate to the point of feeling puzzled about who we are. That's what has happened to me in the past – I've ended up feeling like I'm in a cage that I want to break out of. When I look back, I can see that I helped to create my own cage by not being fully myself.

In my relationship with Jenny, we've spoken about what would happen if one of us wanted to leave the relationship. We've both admitted that it would be gut-wrenching, but that we would let each other 'go' without any unfelt feelings being projected onto the other. We've also agreed that, in the event of a breakup, we would stay together for two months to grieve and close the relationship in a loving way. That's a commitment we will honor no matter what.

One last thing I'll share with you about our relationship. We've both got a celebrity pass! If you don't know what that is, here's how the Urban Dictionary defines it –

A celebrity free pass is an agreement between you and your significant other that if you meet said celebrity and there is an opportunity to sleep with them, your partner cannot get mad at you for doing so because you had agreed beforehand that this person was your celebrity free pass. It is ideal if both of you in the relationship choose a celebrity free pass so that the playing field is even.

It appears, however, that both of us may be slightly deluded, because there aren't many celebrities queueing up to have one-night stands with us! But we can have a good laugh about it because we don't want to take ourselves too seriously. As our egos let go of any ideas of control or manipulation, we reveal our deepest selves to each other, confident of the loving embrace of the other, no matter what. That loving embrace transforms the fear of being seen into the excitement and wonder of revelation. We now know that we can stretch into the unknown. We can stretch our minds, our hearts and our bodies, beyond what they knew previously. It makes love a journey, not a destination. Once that is grasped by the mind, then the journey opens into the heart and the body – and you help each other to become whole. This is the deeper purpose, function and meaning of relationship.

Our relationship inspired me to write a poem about it:

Snug
We are
snug,
together,
like slippers on a Christmas morning –
soft-stepping down the stairs,
our childhood years
still chestnut warm in our hands
touching
briefly,
as we linger on the bottom step –
somehow wrapped together
in the unashamed honesty
of our separate lives,
each one a mystery
to the other,
each one unfolding
within the embrace of the other,
reveling
in being revealed.

And now
we are moving,
easily,
towards breakfast,
alive with the oxygen
of the years of seeking,
so we could meet
ourselves
and each other,
sensing the sacred –
in the dog yawning,
in the coffee brewing,
in the acknowledgment
of us,
snug,
together,
like slippers on a Christmas morning.

This snugness is a very different feeling to that heady phenomenon of falling in love. As you probably know, we see the best in the other person at the beginning. Give it six months or so and we start seeing other aspects we hadn't noticed before. After a while longer we wonder how we could have been so blind!

That had been a pattern for both myself and Jenny, so when we met, we decided to be 100% open and honest from Day One. Rather than try to impress by putting our 'best face' on, we began our relationship by telling each other, very openly and honestly, what we were like at our worst! Yes, we did that in our first week! It's probably not for everyone, but it worked for us.

Over the years both of us have changed hugely, and thankfully, we both welcome that. We are both free to explore our own development and to include the other as little or as much as we want. We have no expectations of each other except complete honesty. We both have a desire to connect with the sacredness and beauty in the other at the soul level as well as the physical level. We do this through our own unique development of practices and rituals which work for us. The most recent one is that we light a candle and sit for ten minutes in silence with each other in the morning. When we open our eyes we tell each other three things we deeply appreciate about the other. It's very simple and very powerful at the same time.

I know that I would never have grown so much as a person without being with Jenny in this conscious relationship. All I need from her is this: that she continues to discover herself at deeper and deeper levels, and let me witness that and share in that. I am in awe of that process. With Jenny, I feel a deepening in love, not a falling in love. It's different. I told her a few months ago that I was more in love with her than when we met, and that's because we have both changed and grown so much, because of our openness and willingness within our relationship.

Here's how open we are with each other. A few months ago we were in our sumptuous bedroom, which we have co-created in rich and vibrant colors. We had only just opened our eyes, experiencing that warm snuggly time before you're fully awake. Then she said something to me. She said, "I love waking up beside you in the morning, and falling asleep beside you last thing at night." She also said two other lovely things – but while I'm all about openness, I do have a healthy respect for boundaries and privacy, so I'll keep them private!

Back to the scene. After Jenny said those lovely things to me, I didn't feel anything. I didn't believe her. We continued to cuddle and then I stopped, because I just had to express what was going on for me. I said to her, "You said that you love waking up beside me in the morning... and so on... but right now, I can't feel any love in those statements. I don't feel anything. I feel closed."

Many years ago I would have said nothing at all. Or I would have phrased it differently. I might have said, "I don't believe you," or even "I think you're pretending – it didn't feel real for me." If you say something like that, the person you're with will most likely respond with something like, "How dare you say that? Of course I was being truthful…" or maybe even, "Are you calling me a liar?" The 'war' would start – and that would mean that my mind would be justified and satisfied that it was right. My belief that she didn't really love me would be vindicated and strengthened. That's how tricky our ego-self is. It's what happens when the unconscious parts of us are acting out in our relationships, causing drama and disconnection. When we're not even aware of the unconscious it's hard to take responsibility for our own feelings and so we project onto others.

These days, however, I am more in tune with my side of everything, so I decided to lie there and sense into what was going on. I wanted to know what was true for me. I felt into my body and breathed into the sensation of being closed to her love. After a while I said to her, "I wasn't able to feel the love behind those statements. I feel hard, like a wall. I feel closed, cold. It feels like your love can't reach me." I kept on breathing into the sensation of being hard, being closed and having a wall around me. After a while, I felt like a very young child, possibly younger than a year old. I had a sense of needing the reassuring touch of love but it wasn't forthcoming. Then I realized that I had rejected my neediness by putting up a wall around me. Somewhere in my psyche I had decided that I didn't want to feel any rejection or loneliness feelings ever again. So I buried them behind that hard wall I was now sensing into. I began to understand that, somewhere along the way, I had made the situation mean something about me as a child, something like, "Eoin, you're not really loveable just as you are." It seems that I had been carrying that around with me for a long time.

However, now that I am a reasonably conscious adult, I'm able to use moments like these to name what's actually going on without blaming anyone for anything. So I said to Jenny, "I can feel a sense of needing love, not getting it, and then feeling a sense of rejection. There's sadness there too, and a bit of rejection and loneliness."

As I lay there I began to feel into the constriction in my heart chakra. As I kept breathing into the cold protective layer the hardness began to thaw and melt. Some gentle tears arrived. Jenny kept quiet beside me all this time, being a loving presence and witness to what was going on, without trying to fix it or offer solutions. This is what we do for each other when it's needed. This is genuine authentic honest love.

When the energy had cleared I was able to see how I was still protecting myself at times from a deeply honest connection with my partner, whom I love very much. Rather than allow myself to feel the deep love she has for me, I was still trying to keep it at bay, by closing up, by telling myself that her love wasn't real. Not all the time, of course, but subtly allowing myself to feel separate at times and unconsciously blaming her. To put it another way, I didn't want to feel the possibility of rejection, so I wouldn't allow her love in. While the wall around my heart is much smaller than it used to be, it was still subtly there as a protection. But it also kept her love out to some degree. That way, I would never feel rejected or lonely again when she wasn't able to love me exactly when I wanted it. No partner can be absolutely unconditionally loving all the time! We're all human.

That's what the mind does with any feeling that's still held within you. You're completely unaware of the feeling itself, because you weren't able to process it when you were very young. Your body has closed off from it, and then something external triggers it. It begins to activate, but of course, you don't like the feeling. To make sense of what's happening then, the mind says: "It can't be to do with you. It must be his or her fault that you're feeling this way."

Our ego-mind will not make itself wrong in any way, so it makes the other person 'wrong.' This is called projection, one of our strategies for avoiding our own feelings. These unfelt feelings grow into beliefs that protect us from feeling the pain that arose in the first place. Let's say you were betrayed in a previous relationship. Then you meet someone wonderful, but the residue of the previous relationship hasn't been dealt with. You live your life with the unconscious belief that "Men are untrustworthy." All your interactions with a new partner are tainted by this unconscious belief. He may be the most trustworthy guy on the planet, but it doesn't matter. Your mind has taken a fixed position which it won't release until you challenge it, in you. You've got to dive into your heart and allow yourself to feel all the feelings still hanging around since the previous betrayal.

Remember, please, that feelings are just feelings. We don't need to be scared of them. When you deeply allow yourself to feel everything you need to feel, every day can bring something new, a revelation, a challenge, a surprise. The beauty of being able to work within the present moment and go deep into it is this – you gradually free yourself from all the unconscious luggage, wounds and old energy patterns that you're carrying around with you. You begin to recognize what I call the "Strategic Self" which runs your life for you most of the time, until you catch on to it. Yes, it's challenging to be truly authentic. Yes, it's frightening to the ego that wants you to hold onto your idea of how the world is, how he or she is, how men are, how women are – and so on. But if you're truly on a spiritual journey you've got to use your relationships to teach you about your projections, your edges, your walls. You've got to learn to let the love in.

You can trust that, at your center, you are love. You love to love and be loved. At the deepest level of reality, you are life and love itself, growing every day in the womb of creation. Most of us never connect in with ourselves at this level. You may have caught glimpses of it in a peak experience where you broke through some hardness or constriction or healed an old wound. This is a temporary expansion. Afterwards you fall back into yourself, and the experience gets lost in the fabric of our everyday lives. We tend to forget, on a regular basis, that we are this love – because on an equally regular basis, the world is showing us the absence of love.

If, in our first few weeks on earth, our bodies were not held and nurtured with infinite tenderness, patience and warmth, then we felt the lack of that on a physical level. As we grew older we carried that wound into our adult lives, and many of us now find that we desperately desire and need loving human touch. As children we had no protection against the harshness of the world we found ourselves in. We could not embody the love that we were. The only strategy that worked was to close down. It was our only refuge, and so we developed ways of closing off from anything painful in the world we found ourselves in. When you're very young, you experience and interpret the world through the body, because you lack emotional or intellectual intelligence. And so, it is the body that registers the pain. It is the body that closes down first, followed by our hearts and our minds. While we are born as beings of love, the world that we are born into does not reflect back to us our true nature of love. We grow up seeing our parents and others as giants whose job it is to mirror that love back to us, so that we know who we are. But quite often these 'giants' don't show unconditional love to us, at least not all of the time. Most of us were not born to enlightened parents. They criticize us. They shout at us. They threaten us. They place high expectations on us. They control us.

When, as small children, we are criticized by these 'giants,' we believe that we are faulty in some way. We don't have the strength or resources to question what the giants are saying or doing – and so naturally enough we believe that they are right and therefore we are wrong. They are right to criticize us, to judge us, to shame us, and be angry at us – and we are somehow wrong, defective, not good enough – take your pick from a long list! Unfortunately many of these thoughts become hardened in our psyche and they gather 'weight' from constant repetition and reinforcement. The more weight they gather the more they bury that love inside, and we end up as a hotchpotch of what was presented to us by life, masquerading as functional or even successful adults. A lot of the time we're just going through the motions and pretending, because we're too scared to look inside, afraid of what we might find. But if you're brave enough to keep on looking, you'll get to your core. What you'll find there is pure love, honest, open, raw and authentic love.

It Felt Love – Hafiz
How
did the Rose
ever open its Heart
and give to this World
All its
Beauty?
It felt the encouragement of Light
against its Being,
Otherwise,
We all remain
Too
Frightened.

Chapter 16

Demons and Archetypes

The demon that you can swallow gives you its power,
and the greater life's pain, the greater life's reply.
– Joseph Campbell

In his book *The Hero with a Thousand Faces*, Joseph Campbell identified the elements of what he called The Hero's Journey. Most of our fairy tales and many movies have this archetypal journey at their core. In simple terms, the journey goes through three stages –

1 Departure/The call to Adventure
2 Initiation/Temptations/Trials/Demons/Monsters
3 The Return

The same story is being retold over and over again in our own lives, and it is also the story of Odysseus, of Dorothy, Luke Skywalker; Braveheart and Harry Potter too. It is the journey of the Buddha and of the Christ. If you're still thinking in dualistic terms, you'll recognize it as the eternal struggle between Good and Evil. If your thinking has moved to beyond right and wrong, you'll see it as the quest for self-actualization, for enlightenment.

Though these questions ultimately drive our lives, we often ignore the call. We're too busy. We don't have the money. We don't believe we can really achieve freedom, and make our dreams come true. We're too afraid. But the fact remains that we are all called to do the work we were born to do, and to self-actualize. Some of us are aware that we're on a journey, and some are totally unaware.

And, just like Neo in *The Matrix*, we're all ordinary people. We only become heroes because we can't ignore the call any longer, and set out on our journey. We embark on a grand adventure where we'll meet challenges, temptations, demons – and our greatest fears. Like Frodo in *The Lord of the Rings*, we know we're not strong enough for the journey, but we also know that we don't have an option. Once we start, we can't stop. Something is calling us, and we somehow know that we'll get lots of support on the way.

During the journey, we will be confronted by our demons and our greatest fears. They will show up in the ordinary aspects of our lives, in our health, our finances, our relationships. We will be taken to the edge of our capacity, time and time again. It won't always be easy, but ultimately, like the heroes in our stories, we keep going. Why? Because the rewards are huge, and the journey is exhilarating. Just like Moses, we are leaving slavery and striking out for the Promised Land! Along my journey to my own Promised Land, I met many demons. Here's how I met The Victim, and what I learned at that time.

After my marriage ended my two sons lived with me, and my two daughters lived with their mum, about a two-hour drive away – and I provided for both families. A few years later, my daughters, now 12 and 17, decided to live with me, and my ex-wife moved to Spain. I was very resentful when I didn't get any financial support from her. After all, I had supported them when it was the other way around. My mind began to weave a whole story around this. I ended up with a looping narrative that said, "She should pay some support for her children," and I told anyone who cared to listen how hard done by I was. At the time I didn't recognize that my victim consciousness was awakening, and that I was building up more and more resentment in myself. However, I was lucky enough to come across a wonderful process called "The Work" by Byron Katie, where she gets you to question your thoughts in a very powerful way. If you want to look it up, pop onto thework.com.

Using "The Work" I questioned my constant thought – "She should pay some support for her children." My AHA moment came when I got to Stage Three of the process, which comes in two parts:

(a) How do you feel when you believe that thought?
I wrote down, "I feel angry, frustrated, powerless, disappointed."

(b) Who would you be without that thought?
"I would be lighter, easier in myself, freer."

Then I got to Stage 4, which she calls The Turnaround. Here you simply turn the thought into its opposite, and see how that thought affects how you feel. So I turned it into a few different 'thought options' like – "I should support my children." Result? I felt appreciative that I was able to support them.

"Not every parent supports their children." Result? I felt better about myself.

"She shouldn't support her children." Result? I laughed! I realized that I could think any thought I wanted, and that if I was thinking a thought that caused me to feel 'angry, frustrated, powerless and disappointed,' then I was doing that to myself. What a revelation. I loved it! I saw very deeply that I had the power to make myself feel anything, depending on the way I was thinking. So I kept thinking new thoughts about the situation, just to feel better in myself. The situation you're in may never change, but at least your experience of it is now controlled by you. So I thought some new thoughts: "I love supporting my children... I love taking care of them as best I can... I love that I get to spend all this time with them." I ended up being very appreciative of what I had, rather than resentful over what I didn't have!

The Victim was a part of me that I hadn't realized was there at all. It was in my unconscious, and it only awakened when these particular circumstances arose. That's what happens on the journey. According to Jung, we all must become aware of what's in our unconscious, especially the parts of ourselves that we refuse to acknowledge. If we try to repress or deny, ignore or flee from these parts, they will keep growing and gain even more power from us.

Imagine you're swimming along, and you have a beach ball that you don't want anyone to see. You've got to keep it underwater, but the more you press down on it, the more it wants to jump up and be seen by the world. That's what the shadow is like. First, you need to accept that it's there, rather than try to hide it. You need to integrate it into your psyche. If, for example, you feel powerless, frustrated or resentful a lot of the time, or are afraid of confrontation, then you probably have anger in your shadow. You don't like angry people. You see anger as something bad, because you've experienced it in an unhealthy way when you were little. But anger has a lot of positives to it. In my life, it helps me to self-motivate, to be very clear in what I'm saying and to set appropriate boundaries. Gandhi is one example of a man who used his anger very positively. He said, "I have learned... to conserve my anger and (as heat conserved is transmitted into energy) anger controlled can be transmitted into a power that can move the world." If you meet your Anger Demon, you'll be afraid of it. Your job is to gradually befriend it and integrate the power of its anger so that you can be a more powerful person. In *The Lord of the Rings*, for example, Sam must 'become terrible' and behave in a most unhobbity manner, by allowing himself to feel the power of his anger and use it to fight Shelob and rescue Frodo from Cirith Ungol.

Gollum, of course, is Frodo's shadow. He represents Frodo's biggest fear, that he will succumb to the temptation of the Ring's siren call. Frodo fears and despises Gollum until the moment he actually sees him clearly. When he sees Gollum in the light of day, he experiences compassion. This is wonderfully symbolic for us as we acknowledge our shadow, forgive ourselves and become whole. As I continued on my own journey, I began to see that all of my demons were like little lost parts of me, all wanting my attention, my understanding and my love. I learned to greet all the pattern of energy in my psyche, the angry monster, the poor-me victim, the manipulative liar, the opinionated evangelist and the controlling dictator.

Here's a deeper look at two of them:

The Evangelist: "I believe in whatever I believe in, and you should also. I dedicate my life to making others believe what I believe. Then I can feel good about my belief. If you don't believe, then you're not part of my gang!"

People can be incredibly evangelical about almost anything... Yoga, Religion, Atheism, New Age, Raw Food, Vegetarianism, Politics. For some extreme versions it goes further, "My belief says that if you don't believe what I believe, I have the right to kill you."

The Victim: "Poor me," it says, "look at me, I've had a really hard life, please understand me. Yes, I am down in this hole... but you're up there having a great life, you're really lucky... why don't you help me... oh no, I'm not sure I want a hand-up, maybe you could throw some food down to me, it's easier down here; I don't have to take any real responsibility and I can complain and moan all the time. You won't believe what the last person said to me. How dare they! If I was up there, I wouldn't complain at all. You sure have it easy, all of you."

Later on, I came across the concept of archetypes through the wonderful work of Caroline Myss, building on the work of Carl Jung, the great Swiss psychologist. For Jung, archetypes comprised psychological patterns derived from historical roles in life, such as the Mother, Child, Trickster, and Servant. Along with our personal and individual unconscious, Jung asserted, "there exists a second psychic system of a collective, universal, and impersonal nature that is identical in all individuals." This collective unconscious, he believed, was inherited rather than developed, and was composed mainly of archetypes. Some are easier to understand than others. Mother, for example, is a universal archetype. When we say the word Mother we know what we mean by it. Child. King. Lover. Fool. These are all familiar archetypes that we use in our everyday language. "She's a real princess." "He was her white knight." "She's a rescuer."

Carolyn Myss says that we all have to transcend the victim archetype in order to move into authentic power. As I looked at a checklist for the inner victim, I recognized myself in many of the statements. That awareness helped me to really get to know myself and finally transcend any residue of victim that I was still carrying. Have a look and see if any of these statements resonate with you, whether you think them or say them out loud.

Victim Statements

He/she needs to change.

Look what you made me do.

Nobody listens to me.

I'm sick and tired of doing it all.

Can you believe what she did to me?

I don't have enough time.

I can't help it, it's just the way I am.

It's all his/her fault.

You made me feel…

Some people have all the luck.

People always let me down.

Look at all I've done for you.

Nobody appreciates how hard I work.

Someone has to suffer for what happened to me.

It's not my fault.

If I keep feeding them, they'll stay alive. Now, I've gotten used to ignoring them.

– From the movie, *A Beautiful Mind*

Things are only a problem when we don't acknowledge them. It's one of strange things about us humans, that we don't want to face the truth about ourselves. We don't want to acknowledge that a part of us:

- gets off on feeling angry and resentful, rather than feel our rejection wounds;
- takes perverse pleasure in not forgiving, rather than feel our abandonment issues;
- really enjoys bitching about others who "have it made";
- is unable to face into our grief about the relationship breakup;
- justifies our resentment over a past betrayal, and feeds it for years until it turns into bitterness;
- is afraid to get angry, because we might explode. It's easier to pretend we're OK with everything.

There's always some trade-off for us, because it is difficult to acknowledge our own pain. We need to learn to be gentle with ourselves, because the demon doesn't want to be exposed. It will tell you, "This is too hard," and "Don't go there." We need to stay very aware when our awareness is being hijacked again.

Remember what Benjamin Franklin said: "The things which hurt, instruct." The issue for all of us is that when we feel hurt, we don't look for the instruction. We fall in on ourselves, or lash out at the other. While there is an impulse deep inside us to live and create, there's also an equally strong impulse to destroy and to kill. We see it acted out in a whole genre of action and war movies, which then morphed into Xbox and Game Boy 'search and destroy' missions. It appears to be easier for us as a species to be AGAINST something, rather than FOR something. Opposition tends to come rather easily to us, and cooperation seems to be a devalued concept. It doesn't seem to matter what the issue is – you will take sides, somehow. You will be convinced that you're right, and the other side will be equally convinced that they are right. We can take any statement or opinion, and find ourselves in opposition to it. What usually happens is that it then becomes personal, and you both end up 'making the other wrong.' And so the conflict begins, and that deeply hidden impulse to destroy and kill begins to become energized. "I'm right, you are wrong," it screams. The more energized it becomes, the more convinced you are that you are justified and that you are the one who has been wronged. Your ego-mind will latch on to any thought that will feed this monster. Naturally enough, the stronger and more entrenched it becomes, the stronger and more entrenched the 'enemy' becomes too.

You've all seen this in your personal relationships. Everything is going along really smoothly, at least on the surface. But one day your partner comes home and forgets to kiss you. It's been a hard day and he simply forgets to greet you in the usual way. Your demon begins to awaken! It begins to dwell on that little omission. It starts telling you stories about why he has suddenly lost interest. It looks back over the past weeks and sees things in a different perspective. He was late home one day and didn't explain where he was. Was he with someone else? What about that overnight three months ago that he said was forced on him because the plane was cancelled? Was he telling the truth? The stories and questions in your mind grow bigger and more fanciful. Now you're both sitting down to eat and then you start 'leaking' energy. You throw out the veiled comment: "How's that new colleague of yours doing – Fiona, isn't that her name? I hear she's very pretty and a bit of a flirt."

If your partner's demon begins to awaken, then you've got a war, probably a temporary one, but at least your demon has the war it wants. Both demons rise up and take over for a while, and you say and do things that you 'normally' wouldn't. If your partner, however, is very much aware of his 'demon,' he will feel it as it begins to awaken. He may also recognize that you're trying to hook him in to a drama. And so he has a choice.

This is the beauty of doing inner work, because you get to know what's going on at a deeper level. You see that your demon is waking up but, crucially, you don't allow it to take you over.

The issue is that most of us don't recognize that a part of us wants to sabotage what we really want – which is love and acceptance. We can clearly see what's wrong with the other person, but we've never looked in the mirror. This is what Jesus meant when he said: "first remove the log in your own eye, and then you will see the speck of dust in your partner's eye."

Conflict breeds conflict. You will never stop the aggression in the world by being against it. It's already there. Don't add to it. Recognize that you are approaching the problem with the same energy that created it – aggression – and this time it's your own. Take charge of it. Own it. It's yours. Say Hello to it. Recognize it and befriend it.

In my work with people I often get them to use phrases like: "Hello, Anger," or "Hi there, Victim Energy" or "Hello, Dominator and Controller." Naming it creates a little space between you and 'it.' That means you're not projecting it onto the other person. It's yours. If it helps, you can give it a silly name. Some of my internal 'guests' are: Inner Bitch, Raging Warrior, Vacuous Victim, Pretty Polly, Poor-Me-Thingummy, Rebellious Rupert, Calcified Controller! Be careful of taking it all too seriously. Lighten up!

When the demon doesn't have a target to feed off, you can allow it to discharge some of its own energy using any one of a number of practices. The important thing is that you allow yourself to feel what's going on. This is the key to transformation. If you allow yourself to feel the emotion without the story attached to it, you begin the process of de-energizing the demon and building the muscle of awareness. This will ultimately lead you to be free of these triggered and unconscious reactions. You've got to feel all the emotion WITHOUT the story, because it's the story you tell yourself that feeds the demon.

So how do you respond to the problems that continually surface in your life? Can you see them as learning opportunities/solutions-in-waiting? If you're conscious and awake, you will see the energy pattern awakening, but you will not forget yourself. This is what is called being fully present or fully alert. Gurdjieff calls it "self-remembering," while Buddha called it being "rightly mindful" and Krishnamurti preferred "awareness." It's a real gift to be awake to the sensations in our bodies, the feeling in our emotions and the stories in our minds. When we're awake, we listen more to what's going on inside us, as well as what's going on outside. Don't you find it strange that in our 'advanced' society, we have learned to numb ourselves out so that we don't feel. We even take legitimate drugs to stop us from feeling. We also rationalize so that we don't have to listen to our hearts. We dump our anger on the other rather than feel our own. This is all 'normal' behavior.

All of your demons and resulting behavior and emotional patterns are fed by the stories that are repeated in your head. Writing these stories down is a very therapeutic practice. Remember, the stories are not you. They're just stories. Most of us are too ashamed to write down what goes on in our heads, without censorship. On a particular long-term course we (the twelve participants) were all asked to fill one foolscap page with our sexual fantasies and then to notice if we were censoring ourselves. At the beginning, I found myself thinking, "I can't write that down, in case someone else sees it!" My inner censor was quite strong. Eventually, though, I did write them all down and the shame began to dissipate. When we were finished we folded our papers up nice and small, and we put our writings into a paper basket. Then we each picked out a random sheet of paper and read it out to the group! Yes, out loud, to the group! Initially I had thought that my fantasies were shocking, but not so. The others were far more shocking to me! We all laughed a lot that day, and with the laughter came a huge release of shame. It appears that we're all equally disturbed or, if you like, equally normal!

The act of writing without censorship is very powerful. Instead of listening to all our demons we can write what they're saying. When I began to do 'morning pages' (from Julia Cameron's book *The Artist's Way*) I was amazed at what flowed out of my head and onto the page. Yet again I was shocked by what went on in my head! After a few weeks I realized that, even though no one else was going to see what I had written, I was still holding back. I was still censoring the words. I finally committed to not censor anything – and to allow ANYTHING that was in my mind to come out onto the page. Some of it was dark. Very Dark. Scary Stuff. Vengeful. Spiteful. Resentful. Sadomasochistic. Dominant. Sexual. Angry. Judgmental. Some of it was very creative. Some of it was wonderfully light.

Overall, though, it was cathartic. It felt like I was spring cleaning. As the weeks passed the garbage all went onto the page. Every week I would look back at what I had written, note any recurring theme that I felt I had to do some work on, and then, in a little ritual, I would burn the pages. After eleven weeks I woke up one morning and started my normal stream of consciousness practice. But it wasn't the usual repetitive garbage. It was the beginning of a story. I was a 12-year-old girl, and I was leaving home! I'll never forget that morning, because it showed me what happens when we empty out the old.

You make space for something new. As I deepened in my practices and continued on my journey, I was finally seeing the amazing benefits of all the practices I had been through. Sometimes you've just got to stop wallowing in the stories that feed your demons. You've got to get up off the chair, or put the wine away, or switch the TV off. You've got to do something different, otherwise, you'll end up doing the same over and over again. It's easy to fall into repetitive ways of thinking, feeling and behaving.

When I'm working with a client, and I see that the same tears are being shed over and over again, I ask, "Do those tears serve you?" This is not a lack of empathy. It's a recognition that people can get stuck in the Yin emotions, like sadness and power-lessness, rather than go deeper and feel the more powerful Yang emotions underneath, like anger.

Other people can feel the yang emotions quite easily, and get stuck in their anger or justification. They're afraid to open up the deep hurt and vulnerability underneath the anger. People who feel their anger quite easily usually have powerful voices that need to be heard, because they can be terrified of silence, or doing nothing. They're afraid of any space that would open their feelings of vulnerability, and so they maintain a strong ego personality which seeks to convince others that they're strong. They may look like successful politicians, teachers, orators, self-proclaimed experts – but underneath all that bravado and bluster is, usually, a frightened child.

Whatever emotion you fear, whether it's your vulnerability or your anger, will control your experience of life. The fear of being honest about what's going on inside you will always close you down, so that nobody gets to see the real you. Looking at it from the standpoint of spirituality and deep presence, however, emotion is actually our teacher and our friend. We learn to watch the emotion as it courses through our body, but we don't lose our presence, our inner core. We know that it's just an emotion, and that this too will pass. It will pass much more quickly if you don't feed it a story. If you're feeling resentment, for instance, remember that you feed it if you replay a narrative or story in your head. But if you don't replay that story, and step back a little, you can watch the resentment die. You don't resist it, and you don't feed it. You simply watch it, and it will die. If you've built up layers and layers of a particular emotion, it will take some time to unravel it all. All you have to do is be patient, notice what triggers you, and what emotional reaction has become your norm. Whether you're disappearing into blame and powerlessness, passive or aggressive controlling behavior, or simply closing off altogether, you need to recognize that this behavior pattern may have begun to define your very identity.

In school you get the lesson and then take the test...
In life you take the test and then get the lesson.
– Unknown Source

Underneath it all, the true you begins to emerge, akin to being 'born again.' Your soul wants to become whole now, bringing together the opposing forces at work within you. This is spiritual alchemy and radical transformation. You are letting go of every single thought, belief or energy pattern that has been crucifying you, because, just like Jesus on the cross, you have a Christ-self, a Shekinah, a Soul-Self seeking to express itself through you. And just like Jesus, your Christ-self is calling you to let the 'old you' be crucified. If someone looks for the old you (as the women did after Jesus' death) they'll find the tomb empty. Your old self is not there anymore, or more correctly, your old ego-self is not there anymore. The real You has been resurrected.

The old story, about how the butterfly needs to struggle before it emerges whole from the cocoon, illustrates this perfectly.

A young boy was playing in the garden and found a caterpillar. He picked it up and brought it home, as young boys do! He asked his mother if he could keep it in a jar, and she agreed. He put plants to eat, and a stick to climb on, in the jar, and watched the caterpillar every day. One day the caterpillar climbed up the stick and started doing something new. The boy called his mother, who explained to the boy that the caterpillar was making a cocoon, and would go through a metamorphosis to become a butterfly.

The little boy was excited! He watched day after day, as the caterpillar stayed in the cocoon, doing nothing. Eventually, a small hole appeared in the cocoon and the butterfly started to struggle to come out. Hours went by. The butterfly was struggling so hard to get out! It looked like it couldn't break free! It looked desperate! It looked like it was making no progress! The boy was worried, and decided to help. He got a scissors and carefully snipped the cocoon to make the hole bigger. The butterfly emerged instantly!

As the butterfly came out the boy was surprised to see it had a swollen body and small, shriveled wings. He continued to watch it, expecting that, at any moment, the wings would somehow dry out, enlarge and expand, so that the butterfly could fly. But it didn't happen! The butterfly spent the rest of its life crawling around with a swollen body and shriveled wings, not able to fly. It never developed the beautiful colors on its wings either.

The boy's mother gave him a science book which explained it all. The butterfly was **SUPPOSED** to struggle. The struggle to push its way through the tiny opening of the cocoon would have pushed the fluid out of its body and into its wings. Without the struggle, the butterfly would never ever fly.

So, whenever you're struggling, remember that the struggle itself is there to help you develop into something beautiful!

Exercise – Emptying Out

Write out three completely uncensored blank pages. Don't let the pen stop.

Do this every day for a week, first thing in the morning. Be very curious about what you find. Remember not to judge the content of our mind. It is what it is.

Chapter 17

Anger, Energy and the Future

Letting go is an act of freedom,
because no one has bound you,
except perhaps yourself.
– Eoin Scolard

I didn't do anger very well in my family of origin, nor afterwards, as a parent and husband in my own family. I guess most families don't do anger well, partly because of the negative press that this powerful emotion gets, and partly because we don't have the skills to know when to contain it, and when to express it in a nondestructive way. It took me about 48 years of day-to-day living on this planet before I began to understand what anger was really about, and what it was telling me. Up to that point, I had a difficult relationship with anger and so I didn't handle anger well with my own children. This is what happens until we evolve beyond what was handed down to us. There's no blame in any of this. We simply don't know any other way – until we do!

As a young child I experienced the anger of my parents, teachers, other adults, my friends and all my siblings. Some of us were marched into the kitchen when we did something wrong. The dreaded wooden spoon lay lurking in a drawer there, ready to sting my young fingers if I stepped out of line. The teachers at school had canes which belonged in locked cupboards, and the so-called Christian Brothers had straps hanging from their belts, like phallic representations of their suppressed sexual power. I'm still not sure which I dreaded more when I knew I had been a bad boy – having to wait for the punishment, or the act itself. Even the sounds made me suck my breath in as I stood there, waiting. The whoooosh of the cane as the teacher limbered up. Me trying to pull my fingers out of the way at the last minute and take the cane on my hand instead. The rattle of the wooden spoon drawer as my mother reached in, and then the quick, hard thwat of the wooden spoon across my palms. Left. Right. The 'Brother' undoing his leather belt with obvious relish and the dull splat as the belt contacted the soft skin on my bottom. It always felt worse when you had to sit down in the classroom afterwards. It seems that we were all bold children and that this was the only way we would learn.

I learned the lesson quickly, associating power and authority with anger, which I saw as a negative force. I began with being afraid of anger and then made the small jump to being afraid of arousing anyone's anger. I had to behave and be a good boy, a nice boy, and that became my norm. I learned not to speak up in case I awakened someone's anger. As a teenager, I often felt angry about my freedom being constricted, but didn't allow myself to fully express it. So I huffed and puffed or lied instead, rather than directly confront the authority being imposed on me. Anger can be very well disguised within us. Most of us are disconnected from it and need some guidance to unearth it and make friends with it, so that we can use it constructively in our lives.

Listening to your own self-talk may give you a clue. One of my clients was always low in energy, and said to me that she was fed up with being tired all the time. "I'm sick and tired of being sick and tired" is what she finally came up with. I reflected back to her that the way she said it felt very powerless. "Well," she said, "I do feel powerless when I think about it."

I suggested to her that she stop thinking about it, and then I dropped the bombshell. "Chloe," I said, "when you say that you're sick and tired, it's possible that, underneath the powerlessness, there's a lot of anger, but you don't know how to channel that productively. You're more used to feeling powerless, which is a feeling you're very familiar with." As we breathed into the powerlessness she felt as a child, Chloe began to touch into the raw anger of her adult self too, about what had happened to her. When I finally got her to say, "It wasn't OK," her anger became her liberator, her friend. She was then able to use the anger to forge the changes she needed to make in her life. There was a whole series of revelations for Chloe. First, that she was angry. Second, that it was OK to feel angry. Third, that we could harness a huge amount of energy from her unfelt anger, and use it in healthy ways.

It's very useful to look at your relationship to anger and power, particularly when you meet with authority as an adult. Your reaction will usually be linked to how you responded to punishment when you were a child. If you were punished for 'talking back' then you probably found some power in less obvious ways, like being late, not doing the homework properly, or acting out against younger children in your family or friends. If you always complied and withdrew into yourself, then you may exhibit passive-aggressive behavior as an adult. Your sense of self can end up being built on trying to please everyone as you attempt to live up to their expectations, making sure to avoid any confrontation or criticism.

Sometimes the anger arises not because your boundary is being crossed, but when your need is not being met. I remember learning this clearly when my youngest daughter was about 15. I was busy juggling with the pressures of single parenting, running a business and holding down a new relationship. Each time I opened the door into her bedroom I could feel the anger rising. You know how it is with teenage bedrooms! When I saw the mess in her room my anger would rise up in a rush and I'd come out with some choice phrases! She'd shrug her shoulders as most teenagers do, and I'd leave the room fuming while she breezed on through the day. After a few episodes of this I realized that my approach wasn't working. I remembered the wonderful work of Marshall Rosenberg in Nonviolent Communication, where he brings you through a four-step process.

In step 3 he says that anger will arise when your need is not being met. I jump to "I need her to clean the room!" but of course that's not it. It has to be MY need. It's nothing to do with my daughter or her room. As I tuned in I realized that I did have a need. I needed to feel supported. Saying that to my daughter felt very vulnerable and I shed a few tears as I told her. She did too.

While opening up to my need was extremely revealing and vulnerable for me it was also immensely powerful, because it opened up a deeper relationship too. It's important to be able to express your need as well as your anger – and here's the trick, never to make it about the other person. In my situation I was able to say to my daughter, "When I can't see the floor in your bedroom I feel frustrated and disappointed because I have a need to feel supported. What I'd like us to do is to clean up your room together once a week, and we'll even play YOUR music while we're doing it!"

Another way of tuning in to yourself in these situations is to notice what your body language is. Do you feel a tension in your mouth and jaw? Do you hold your fists in a clenched position sometimes? Do you feel a weight on your shoulders, the pressure of expectations? If you do, then have a look at this simple checklist and see if your behavior shows classic symptoms of hidden anger –

- Do you take on too much, especially for others – and never get things finished? Are you a master of procrastination?
- Do you often arrive late for meetings and appointments?
- Do you never have enough time?
- On the surface you're always calm, but you don't allow yourself to feel your anger, and so you don't experience much joy either.
- You enjoy sarcasm, cynicism, and/or flippancy.
- You keep attracting partners that seem to have 'anger problems' – but you don't realize that they're simply

mirroring your anger, which is in 'shadow.'
- You are always polite and cheerful, and you minimize any difficulties or challenges in your life. "That's life," you say – while still smiling.
- Your voice is quite controlled and monotonous, with a tight jaw and mouth.
- You are very irritable and impatient – over things that don't really matter.
- In an argument, it's important for you to prove you're right.

It's good to know that your anger will take care of you if you let it. Healthy anger sets healthy boundaries and allows you the freedom to be yourself. When the lioness roars at the grizzly for being too close to her cubs, do we point to her and say she has an anger problem? No, of course not. Anger will look after whatever needs protecting in you. Most of us have an inner child in our psyche, a vulnerable child that needs to feel safe. Anger and vulnerability need to be allowed to coexist within you, without identifying with either end of that spectrum. What we need is the ability to contain, not suppress, our emotions, at the same time as finding ways to allow them to be healthily expressed.

That's not always easy, as I discovered when my anger came to the surface very powerfully in my late thirties. One of the recent patterns in my life at that stage was that whatever car I owned was stolen every now and then, usually once or twice every few years. Each time I would smile and say it wasn't an issue, keeping a calm and reasoned voice. I'd be very logical too, saying that the insurance would cover the damage. Little did I know that, underneath the calm and reasoned exterior, I was very pissed off!

A year later I remember being quite blasé when the doorbell rang at 4am one morning and two police officers told me that my car had been stolen and crashed into the roundabout on the main road. I shrugged as if it wasn't an issue.

"We were chasing them at high speed," said the younger one, her eyes still carrying some of the adrenaline from the chase.

"Yeah, they lost the back end at about 80 miles an hour, slammed sideways into a telegraph pole and then bounced onto the roundabout," said the older man.

"Oh well," I said, "we can't do anything about it, so I suppose I'll go back to bed now."

"No, no, you need to get the car off the roundabout," said the younger one.

I took a step back. "Me? At 4am? Move the car? You just told me it's not drivable."

"You're right, it's not drivable. But it is your responsibility to have it moved. I can give you the emergency number of the tow truck people."

I looked at both of them in disbelief. "So my car was stolen out of my driveway, you guys gave chase, it crashed into the round-about, and I'm supposed to pay for a tow truck!"

"Yes well," she said, "that's just the way it is. You see, the car is half on the roundabout and half on the main road. It will cause an obstruction once the rush hour starts. We just have to get it moved."

"Well," I said triumphantly, "that's your problem. I can get it done later on today, or you can get it done now if you have to."

The older man smiled a little as his younger colleague recognized she had been outmaneuvered.

That was the last incidence of theft I experienced in my calm and reasoned way. The next incident blew the lid off that pent-up anger and frustration, and showed me how dangerous it is to keep bottling it up. That so-called red mist is real!

I guess it was about six months later. I was at a barbecue party at my brother-in-law's house with about 30 others. We were all enjoying the last rays of the Sunday evening sun when a voice called out from beyond the garden wall, "Hey, Mike, are you in there? Someone's stealing your car."

Three of us reacted instantly, including Mike. We vaulted the six-foot high wall that surrounded the property, scanning the road as we dropped to the pathway. There were cars parked everywhere and there, 200 yards to my right, was Mike's car. Two young men were on lookout duty while the third was inside the car trying to start it.

I started to run. That was the last thing I consciously remember. The red mist descended and calm reasonable Eoin disappeared. Something had snapped inside me and I turned into the Irish version of Terminator, all 5'7" and 10 stone of me! Five minutes later I was being pulled off a young man whose face was red and bloodied. "Give it a rest, Eoin," shouted a voice in my ear, "his face is a mess." I snapped back into consciousness and felt like I had just woken up from a dream. My friends told me that I had sprinted incredibly quickly and gave chase in and out of gardens and cars, and jumping garden walls as if I was a champion hurdler. They just couldn't keep up with me. They told me I caught the slowest of the three thieves and had spread him over the low garden wall, the concrete digging into his back as he tried to fight back. I don't remember catching him and I don't remember hitting him, but when I came to, his hair was in my left fist and my right fist was pummeling his face over and over again. I was shocked. My image of myself as a nice calm person had been shattered. I had no idea that my mind had suppressed these feelings for years and years. That's what happens when we don't allow ourselves to feel what's going on. That's what happens when we gloss over our true feelings and pretend that everything is OK.

Predictably, I unearthed a lot of anger in my personal healing work, sandwiched side by side with resentment, grief and powerlessness. As I learned to move into and through my emotional world, I noticed something else – that my mental world was very judgmental. Even when I cleared my feelings about someone or something, my mind wanted to hold onto a judgment about him or her or me. I would judge myself for judging them, and down the rabbit hole I would go! I tried really hard not to judge anyone at all, not realizing the difference between judgment and discernment. Here's what the *Oxford Dictionary* says:

Judgment: An opinion or decision based on thought, sometimes made by a court.

Discernment: The ability to see and understand people, things, or situations clearly and intelligently.

I now understand that judgment comes directly from my ego-mind, founded on a shadow aspect of myself. Judgment creates more judgment, because it needs something to oppose. Those of us who judge others are afraid to look inside. We deny our own hardness, smugness or feeling of superiority. Judgment disconnects us from the person or persons being judged, and also disconnects us from our own hearts. Discernment, on the other hand, is more of a felt sense, coming from a deeper place. It feels open and it doesn't take sides. It's based on intuition, it informs us and helps us to make good decisions.

I remember one very negative experience I had, many years ago, when I hadn't developed that discernment muscle. I attended a workshop facilitated by a charismatic man who made up his own rules regarding what was healthy for us, the attendees in the group, and also for himself. "Anything goes" was the order of the day, and if you dissented, you were "judging" and you "had work to do." Of course, it's classic cult thinking, where everything is justified. I didn't know what I was getting into, even though I saw that the 'Guru' allowed himself to sleep with many of the lovely but vulnerable women who came for healing. Many 'gurus' don't understand boundaries at all, and they will justify anything in the name of openness, expansion and love. You'll also notice that the women are usually a whole lot younger! Many fall prey to this 'cult consciousness,' where they spiritualize everything. There are no rules except one – don't disagree with the group. Don't talk about boundaries, responsibility and containment. Set yourself free of all restrictions and soar into the high-energy world of love and light and anything goes! Of course I didn't really get all of this until one or two of us in the group began to question some of his methods, with very negative consequences. Let me set the background.

At that stage I had a lot of experience of five rhythms work, which is that body-based dance practice. As I've previously written, the five rhythms (in order) are flowing, staccato, chaos, lyrical, and stillness, and these five rhythms, when danced in sequence, are known as a "Wave." I always enjoyed the end of each dance wave, where the music brings you deep into stillness and meditation, and allows quiet time for integration of whatever was going on for you during the dance. When you've explored and danced through some of your deeper issues, you need the stillness time to settle and integrate the chaotic energies that you may have opened up. It allows containment and closure too.

So, back to the healing workshop. I mentioned to one of the other participants that I had a preference for allowing that quiet time at the end of each day. I remember saying that I didn't think it was particularly healthy to keep delving into issues and opening people up right to the last moment of each day, and then allow them to walk out of the workshop that way. It's not healthy for people to be 'opened wide' energetically, and then left to their own devices. Now that I'm older and wiser, I would handle it differently, but, back then, I had never experienced what Debbie Ford called, "*The Dark Side of the Light Chasers*" in her book of that name.

I didn't know that the woman I had spoken to would bring up what I had said in the group the following day. A good facilitator would have dealt with that in a very open and gentle way, but what happened next was unbelievable. The group facilitator began to attack me. I don't mean physically, but when you are a participant in energy work you rely on the facilitator to protect you and set healthy boundaries. As you're very open and fragile at times, it's very easy to be damaged, particularly when you have invested a lot of trust in the group leader. This group leader got lost in his ego and took it personally, even though I had said nothing directly to him. He turned on me and lambasted me for questioning his methods. Basically, he dumped his anger on me, with phrases like: "How dare you..." Unbelievably, he then invited others in the group to dump on me too. Quite a few of them did, using me as a proverbial black sheep. It went on and on. People said the most ridiculous things like, "You look terrible today," and "I knew you weren't to be trusted." The facilitator called it "taking the hit." You were supposed to take these "hits," which were nothing more than people venting their shadow anger at you. Of course, I should have walked away. It would have saved me a lot of psychological and emotional distress. But I didn't.

Group leaders have enormous responsibility when people put their trust in them. They cannot abuse that trust, as this group leader did. While I stood there shaking, feeling incredibly vulnerable, he abused me, psychologically and emotionally, in front of the group. Light and love? I think not! I did write to this person afterwards but the response I got was very defensive. I never went back to that group or that facilitator. Afterwards I discovered others who had questioned his methods and experienced the same treatment. Some of them were psychologically and emotionally traumatized for years.

The reason I'm telling you this is to ask you to be careful who you work with on your journey. Discern. Ask your intuition before you get sucked into something that may be unhealthy for you. When you start opening up in front of a group, it's a beautiful feeling, as you're suddenly lifted through and beyond your pain. At times you can feel like a God, with immense amounts of light pouring through you. It is addictive – and that's the issue! People can become spiritually addicted to the highs and lows of this kind of work. It's a very dangerous roller coaster which often leaves lives in total chaos.

Remember to check in with your intuition on a regular basis. You do have a wisdom within you. Listen to those inner whispers and nudges. You've got to learn to trust your own wisdom, rather than someone else, whether that's a doctor, counsellor, therapist or healer. This trust of our own wisdom is a quality we need to anchor in our everyday reality. It's a 'NOW' type of feeling which arises from connection with your true nature.

Close your eyes and anchor your feet. Connect with the earth. Breathe into your deep belly while silently speaking the word "Trust." Let your body feel the impact of that word as it travels into every constriction, every tight muscle. Let your shoulders drop. Relax your forehead. Breathe. Open into the depth of the word "Trust," and allow yourself to be enveloped by it. Carry it with you during the day and let it remind you of your deeper nature. "Just for today I trust. I trust my own wisdom. Just for today."

It took me a while to notice the insistent little whispers and to trust my own wisdom. I was too busy THINKING all the time. "That's a fancy new car, I wonder what make it is… Damn, I'll be late for the meeting with all this traffic… I'll look foolish… Mind you, that manager is really full of himself… I can't stand him… and his boss could do with some therapy too… and her, she's a real pain-in-the-ass too." And so on, and on, and on. You know the drill. We all do it. We overthink, especially when we're confronted by a challenge. We don't lean into our innate wisdom.

At one point in my own life I was in a situation where I felt very stuck. I kept on thinking, analyzing and re-analyzing, thinking about it. Thinking about the past. Thinking about how I got here. Thinking about how I'd get unstuck. Thinking about all the what ifs. What would I do if she did this, or if he did that. What might they say if I did that – and on and on.

All my thinking didn't change anything, but it did drain me of energy, day after day, building stress on top of stress. My inner wisdom kept telling me to take some action immediately, but I didn't. I ignored all the nudges and intuition, until the day my body decided it had enough. My body's wisdom said, "You haven't been listening at all. You know what you need to do, but you just won't do it. So here's the deal. I'm going to shut your body down for a while. Maybe then you'll get the message loud and clear."

I was at home that morning, grappling with all my usual internal drama and conflict. All of a sudden, I started to feel very unwell and very afraid. Something big was coming and it didn't feel too good. My energy felt like it was being sucked away by a giant vacuum cleaner underneath me. My legs felt weak. I couldn't stop what was happening. The bad feeling crept into me, sitting inside my body like a patient spider surveying its prey. The most terrifying part of it all was the knowledge that I could do nothing about it. I hated being that vulnerable. Every breath I took made the feeling stronger, and of course, I couldn't stop breathing. Every breath carried it deeper into my body. It was like a one-sided chess game where I had no moves, and the other player, the bad feeling, had plenty. It moved into my chest area, silently taking up residence there, like a lord returning to a manor. My heart was beating very fast, and my temperature rose rapidly. I could feel a sickness entering every space in my body, blithely moving into my arms, my feet, my knees. Everything began to get dark inside. It took away most of the light of my consciousness, and then it crawled up my spine and on into my brain, strangling any connection with my body. My head felt like a lighthouse, but someone was turning down the dimmer switch. There was a big storm coming. I dropped to all fours, my heart rate hitting close to 200 now, my shirt sopping with sweat.

I remember it frame by frame, as if in slow motion. Right now I'm on the floor, on all fours, crawling for help. My vision is beginning to close down. I know it's not long now before my whole world is plunged into darkness. Some strange sounds escape my lips. I am trying to talk. "Wab... wah... weh... wah..." is all I can manage, as a dribble escapes my lips, and then drops to the floor. I crawl a few feet, grunting like a stuck pig. Then I collapse completely. What I can sense, though, is that my body has emptied. Warm urine floods my pajamas. My anal sphincter pushes out whatever was in my bowels. The stench is awful. The last glimmer of light starts to fade. I don't know if my eyes are closed or open, but everything is dark.

I use every ounce of consciousness to crawl to the bedroom, but I can't get there. I stop moving and collapse again, this time in the hall. I am fighting an enormous battle inside now. With IT. The Thing. The Black Hole. I can't hear anything. I can't see, or speak, or even feel my body anymore, but somehow I know I'm still here, hanging in there, hanging on to life. I wonder if this is the end.

Miraculously, there is a part of me that is still conscious. I know that. I'm holding onto that last glimmer of light inside me, trying really hard not to give in. There's still a tiny flame somewhere deep inside me.

I manage to stay there for a while, with the flame, and I hold onto it. It's my only hope. I stay with it until I can breathe a little more. I sense hope. More light. My mind opens a little. My nose registers the awful smell again. My thighs feel the wetness. I don't care. I can feel my legs! Even though my body feels like a desolate wasteland, I am smiling inside, because I feel like a winner. I want to remember this joy, knowing that I'm still alive. Someone has called an ambulance. I'm gonna be OK.

I spent a few days in Intensive Care, with every possible tube and monitor attached to me. The first diagnosis was a stroke. Two days later they changed that to a suspected heart attack. The following day it became – "We're not sure what happened." If you've watched *House*, you'll know what I'm talking about. A lot of medicine is a process of elimination. Twelve days later, the neurosurgeon called me in to tell me that I had a full-blown seizure – a grand mal – and that I was suffering from epilepsy. I was shocked. I asked him, "OK, I can accept the diagnosis of epilepsy if you can tell me how I got it please. When, where and how did it arrive? I didn't have it before this, so I guess there must have been some trigger?"

He couldn't answer those questions and became annoyed with me. He prescribed me tablets, which I refused. Straightaway I told him that I didn't believe I needed tablets. What I needed to do was to stop ignoring my intuition. He kept pressing the point that I "had" epilepsy. I said, "No. What happened to me was the result of three things – all of which I can change. Then I'll be fine." I left the hospital the following day, convinced that my intuition was right. I needed to change three things, that's all. Relationship. Career. Health. No biggies there!

But I did change. I knew what I had to do. Finally I was taking action. Within four months I had quit my business, ended the relationship I was in, and started to get fit. I'm happy to say that I don't "have epilepsy." It's possible that extreme stress triggered the seizure, if that's indeed what it was. This is where our medical systems need a more holistic approach, pointing people towards taking action to change their lifestyle rather than ingesting a barrelful of tablets over a lifetime. Our bodies can only take so much, and if we don't listen to them, they collapse. But if you remove the triggers that caused the collapse, you have a chance. By now, you can tell that my journey into Wisdom was a slow one!

All my thinking and stressing and strategizing landed me in the hospital because I hadn't listened to the deeper knowing in my gut. I began to understand that my mind wasn't interested in my happiness. It was just interested in perpetuating itself. This is the fundamental disconnect that is at the core of most of our dysfunction and so-called complexity. The mind wants to be in control of all the aspects of your life. It does not want you to pay any attention to your being-ness. It thrives on the belief that its opinion is always valid and that it always has a say. Our minds are so much in charge of our lives that we don't even question it. We don't realize that we are not our minds, and that we are creating our own misery. We have forgotten that we are the one watching our thoughts, and that consciousness is the essence of who we are.

Energy

Your being-ness on this planet is a result of two things:

1 The energy that you take in.
2 The consciousness which shapes how that energy is used.

The energy of life is always flowing in two directions, from the earth upwards and from consciousness downwards. It manifests in an infinite number of forms, whether as granite rock, a bubbling river, a forest of trees or a squirrel leaping about in the branches. Or, as you and me. All of these have the properties of life within them – although they are very different expressions of life. You, in the form of a human being, are also an 'expression' of life. You are one of its many faces. To sustain this life you need energy, which you collect from various sources. Your prime resource for energy is the earth, which provides food, water and oxygen. You need the earth to sustain your life because your body is designed to take matter (food) and turn it into energy. That's what nature is also doing all the time, taking matter and turning it into energy. The tree takes water and nutrients from the earth, and powers the process of growth by using sunlight. In the same way, you take water and nutrients (food) from the earth and you power your own growth by your own light, or consciousness. As you develop and ground the higher levels of consciousness your whole energy system begins to optimize itself. Your consciousness does not allow you to continue to mistreat your body in the usual ways – shoving in junk food, overeating, too much alcohol and so on. This is not because you've adopted an evangelical attitude, but because you've developed more of a felt sense of what's right for you. You feel more in touch with the very life force itself that is within you.

It was way back in 1934 when it was first postulated that energy could be turned into matter. This was proven in 1997, when Stanford University physicists used a linear collider and a large number of light particles (photons) to produce matter particles. Light produced particles. A higher vibrational energy was used to create a lower vibrational energy. Another way of putting it is that our thoughts become matter. While it is now scientifically proven that we are energy beings, we don't seem to be aware of what we're doing with our amazingly creative potential. When we think or dream or visualize, we are taking very ethereal energy from the higher planes of light and thought and turning them into matter (earth). Thoughts become things. We know this logically. Ideas for new things or new ways of being are always flooding into our world, in the form of electric cars, solar panels, smartphones, nanotechnology, microsurgery and so on. We know that thoughts create things in the outer world, but we don't pay much attention to the fact that they also produce physiological changes in our inner world. Stressful thoughts have been linked to cancer and heart attacks. Anxious thoughts fire up a constant state of fear, resulting in adrenalin and cortisol flooding our systems, even though there's no actual threat. We're so powerful that we can create different states in our bodies by the way that we think.

A whole universe of infinite potential is waiting to be tapped into – and we can connect into this potential when we become aware of what we're thinking, drop the junk, and give our energy to our dreams and desires. If we want these dreams and desires to manifest in the present, we need our consciousness to be highly calibrated. It's like the seed being planted. It needs the right soil, which takes some time to develop, because most of our dreams actually land in the layers of doubt, fear, belief in lack and so on. When we have emptied ourselves of everything that's in the way, the dreams and desires finally 'land' on fertile ground. We have energetically matched up with the possibilities, and we have created matter in the same way that the Stanford physicists did. In a strange way, we have made the future present. We have created matter here and now – the matter of our dreams – from thought.

Over the centuries we have taken thought and combined it with the physical (wood, mud, stone, oil) to produce mud huts, rudimentary tools, clothing, concrete buildings and roads, airplanes, nanochips, burgers, religions and wars! The thought always comes first. It has to, because we are creators. We cannot NOT create. It is one of our innate qualities – we are always creating, from the top down – from thought in the seventh chakra to matter in the root chakra. When we look at the world through this lens it becomes apparent that the external world we live in is a direct result of all the thought processes that are going on in the world.

Thought is just another form of energy that originates in our crown chakra at the top of the skull. It will always seek ground in the lower chakras, in the same way that electricity or lightning seeks ground in the earth. The whole process of manifestation depends on our thoughts 'hitting the ground' and becoming real in the physical world. This, of course, doesn't happen all the time. Many of our thoughts and dreams seem to get stuck somewhere between our minds and our physical reality. Many of us have thoughts like, "I wish..." But the wishes never become real.

This is because, somewhere along the way, we unknowingly sabotage our dreams when we activate the opposite pole to creation – destruction. Everything has to have an opposite, so it's important to recognize that along with our ability to create, we also have the ability to destroy. Otherwise, when we connect with the deep longing to love and be loved, or to be happy, it would just happen easily and effortlessly. But it doesn't. Recognize that there are two forces at work. Accept that, be patient with it all, and your future will gradually reflect your present, how you think, feel and act in each moment.

How you are today determines how your future will be.

The Future

Recognizing these dual aspects of our lives, the polar opposites of light and dark, conscious and unconscious, creation and destruction, is a very important step in the process of creation. If we can at least understand the forces that are at work in our lives, we can perhaps change. However, if we get stuck in blame or resentment or a 'poor me' attitude, then we are investing our attention and energy in powerless states of being. For example you could experience a life event that your mind interprets with this thought – "That person shouldn't have left me" – and that thought descends into your emotional body. As it does it changes into a lower vibration which we might experience as resentment, depending on whether we turn the energy towards ourselves or towards the other. If we feed this negative emotion with similar thoughts for, say, ten years it gathers so much weight and density that it descends even further, and moves from our emotional body into the physical world – i.e. your body. We are beginning to see that it's possible to manifest a disease that somehow represents the physical embodiment of our suppression, emotion or victim mentality. The best analogy I can offer you is that one thought weighs a gram, and it wears a groove in your mental sphere. As you think it again and again it gathers weight and momentum and therefore descends into your emotional world. The more authority you give this belief the larger the groove it wears in your emotional body, and eventually, by adding one thought (1g) at a time, it becomes so heavy that it 'becomes you.'

It's no longer the emotion of resentment. It is the physical embodiment of resentment. It has grounded itself in the earth, which of course in this case is your physical body.

> The key to abundance is meeting limited circumstances with unlimited thoughts.
> – Marianne Williamson

A similar dynamic is at work when we talk about abundance. Your mind gets involved and you mess up the manifestation because you're TRYING to manifest. Remember that there's no 'efforting' involved. If you find that you are 'trying,' then your mind is involved. Perhaps that's one of your patterns, always trying, always seeking. Drop the trying. Drop the seeking. It's the very energy of grasping for more that keeps us from the simple secrets of manifestation.

Here's an analogy. Imagine your dreams as an airplane. It started a journey up there in the sky, and now it's on its way. YOU are an airport, on the ground, a place that receives planes (dreams). Your plane is getting closer now. It's on the radar. Notice how you feel when you sense into how close it is. Can you believe it? Really? Have you made space for it, so that it can actually land, or is the runway cluttered up with beliefs that will stop it landing? Do you doubt? Do you believe: "I don't really deserve this," or "That only happens for others, but not for me"? Are you one of those who do want it to land, but don't really believe it will? Doubt, fear and negativity will keep it up in the air, and you find yourself always waiting for the manifestation of your dream. But here's the trick – STOP WAITING FOR IT! As Eckhart Tolle wrote, "Give up waiting as a state of mind." When your mind is not waiting for the manifestation, you free it up to land. You've got to know that it's there, available to you – and all you have to do is remove everything that's in the way. The biggest thing in the way is DOUBT. This is when open-ended statements like "The possibility exists…" can really work for you. Your mind begins to open to possibility. The more you open to possibility, the less room there is for doubt. Whether the plane lands or not isn't the issue. The issue is whether you've cleared the runway. If you have to have 'IT' now, the runway is not clear. Control and Grasping are still blocking the way. Can you Surrender? Can you let go into Trust? Can you be Patient enough to allow it to land in divine time, rather than ego-time?

You, my friend, are the same as me – infinite potential. When you finally drop the idea that you 'need' anything at all and move into trusting yourself and your inner knowing, the whole universe will conspire to co-create with you. It can't not do that, because it's the way the Universe is designed. There's already a plan for you, to evolve. All you need to do is cooperate with that. Trust it. Your plane is up there, waiting patiently, and all you have to do is clear the runway so that it can land. Follow your dreams. Remember that they are yours, unique to you. They are there for a reason. They exist on the mental plane already. Your job is to get them to land.

So take another breath and notice one last thing with me. Not only is there a voice in your head speaking, there's also another part of you listening. If you find it difficult to quiet the incessant stream of thought in your head, it may be easier for you to know that you don't have to listen anymore. Let it ramble on and on. As you go deeper and deeper into your center you will eventually realize that you aren't listening, and that you can hear the birds singing. When you stop listening to the monkey mind, you're not feeding it anymore, and so, it will die. It has no ground to land in. The runway is clear now, and the first plane can finally land. There will be many more.

Now you're creating your life experience rather than reacting to life experience. Everything starts to make sense to you. As I said earlier, life energy is always flowing in two directions, from the Earth upwards and from consciousness downwards. Let's refine this a little more. Life is what is going on inside us when the two opposite poles of Earth (feminine) and Consciousness (masculine) meet in our physical bodies. We experience life physically (Earth) and we also experience Consciousness (Spirit Plane). The fusion of these two opposites is expressed by us in many ways, and results in the manifestations of our lives. We manifest our bodies. We manifest our emotions, behaviors, actions, communication, beliefs, visions and so on. Every one of us has a different experience of life depending on how much consciousness we bring to our life.

And that is how powerful we are. WE get to choose our experience of life. What a gift! As I evolve I can see this clearly reflected in my own life. It simply gets better and better. Life seems to be cooperating with me more and more. When we all evolve to the state of consciousness that is called 'enlightened,' this earth will be Paradise. This, here, now will be HEAVEN.

In other words, HEAVEN, EARTH and HELL are the same thing.

It's only (y)our consciousness that makes the difference.

Be gentle
Be well
Be strong
Be flexible
Be YOU!

Chapter 18

No-Mind

A meditative poem to be read out very slowly.
(I suggest you take a breath with each line.)
Take away my name
It is not I –
And take away with it
all my titles and all my learnings
Strip away my story –
that wraps itself –
tightly –
around me.
Take away my concepts
take away my beliefs
Take away my thoughts
of who I was
Take away my dreams
of who I will be.
And even take away
the whisper
of who I might have been
or who I might still be.
Let me jump
from my own foolishness
for it threatens me
by believing that something is against me.
Let me fall under my mind
And let me be surrounded
by the depth of my knowing
Let me feel the cavern inside my body
And the wondrous emptiness of my soul.

I feel myself
sinking
deeper
deeper
What is this
that has no name?
Surrendering all my names
Seeing my story
dissolving behind me
Allowing the whisper of future
to fade
into silence
As I come again
to peace –
in this place
Falling
deeper
into the mystery of
breathing
In
holding on
to nothing –
breathing
Out
Embracing everything –
breathing
In
Letting go of
everything
breathing
Out
Embracing
nothing.
I am open to the sky,

Yet my roof is full of stars.
My roots linger on in the galaxies,
Yet I swim in the ocean that surrounds me.
Breathing In
my absence
Breathing Out
my presence.
Simply sitting –
on my chair,
Surrounded by me
Sitting somewhere
Sitting nowhere
Sitting where you are
Sitting here.
Ah...
Peace...
is where...
I am

BOOKS

O-BOOKS

SPIRITUALITY

O is a symbol of the world, of oneness and unity; this eye represents knowledge and insight. We publish titles on general spirituality and living a spiritual life. We aim to inform and help you on your own journey in this life.

If you have enjoyed this book, why not tell other readers by posting a review on your preferred book site? Recent bestsellers from O-Books are:

Heart of Tantric Sex
Diana Richardson
Revealing Eastern secrets of deep love and intimacy to Western couples.
Paperback: 978-1-90381-637-0 ebook: 978-1-84694-637-0

Crystal Prescriptions
The A-Z guide to over 1,200 symptoms and their healing crystals
Judy Hall
The first in the popular series of four books, this handy little guide is packed as tight as a pill-bottle with crystal remedies for ailments.
Paperback: 978-1-90504-740-6 ebook: 978-1-84694-629-5

Take Me To Truth
Undoing the Ego
Nouk Sanchez, Tomas Vieira
The best-selling step-by-step book on shedding the Ego, using
the teachings of *A Course In Miracles*.
Paperback: 978-1-84694-050-7 ebook: 978-1-84694-654-7

The 7 Myths about Love...Actually!
The journey from your HEAD to the HEART of your SOUL
Mike George
Smashes all the myths about LOVE.
Paperback: 978-1-84694-288-4 ebook: 978-1-84694-682-0

The Holy Spirit's Interpretation of the New Testament
A Course in Understanding and Acceptance
Regina Dawn Akers
Following on from the strength of *A Course in Miracles*, NTI
teaches us how to experience the love and oneness of God.
Paperback: 978-1-84694-085-9 ebook: 978-1-78099-083-5

The Message of A Course In Miracles
A translation of the text in plain language
Elizabeth A. Cronkhite
A translation of *A Course in Miracles* into plain, everyday
language for anyone seeking inner peace. The companion
volume, *Practicing A Course In Miracles,* offers practical lessons
and mentoring.
Paperback: 978-1-84694-319-5 ebook: 978-1-84694-642-4

Rising in Love
My Wild and Crazy Ride to Here and Now, with Amma, the
Hugging Saint
Ram Das Batchelder
Rising in Love conveys an author's extraordinary journey of

spiritual awakening with the Guru, Amma.
Paperback: 978-1-78279-687-9 ebook: 978-1-78279-686-2

Thinker's Guide to God
Peter Vardy
An introduction to key issues in the philosophy of religion.
Paperback: 978-1-90381-622-6

Your Simple Path
Find happiness in every step
Ian Tucker
A guide to helping us reconnect with what is really important in
our lives.
Paperback: 978-1-78279-349-6 ebook: 978-1-78279-348-9

Readers of ebooks can buy or view any of these bestsellers by
clicking on the live link in the title. Most titles are published in
paperback and as an ebook. Paperbacks are available in
traditional bookshops. Both print and ebook formats are
available online.

Find more titles and sign up to our readers' newsletter at
http://www.johnhuntpublishing.com/mind-body-spirit

Follow us on Facebook at https://www.facebook.com/OBooks/
and Twitter at https://twitter.com/obooks